Healthy Kids, Smart Kids

Healthy Kids, Smart Kids

The Principal-Created, Parent-Tested, Kid-Approved Nutrition Plan for Sound Bodies and Strong Minds

Yvonne Sanders-Butler, Ed.D.
with Barbara Alpert

A PERIGEE BOOK

A PERIGEE BOOK
Published by the Penguin Group
Penguin Group (USA) Inc.
375 Hudson Street, New York, New York 10014, USA
Penguin Group (Canada), 90 Eglinton Avenue East, Suite 700, Toronto, Ontario M4P 2Y3, Canada
(a division of Pearson Penguin Canada Inc.)
Penguin Books Ltd., 80 Strand, London WC2R 0RL, England
Penguin Group Ireland, 25 St. Stephen's Green, Dublin 2, Ireland (a division of Penguin Books Ltd.)
Penguin Group (Australia), 250 Camberwell Road, Camberwell, Victoria 3124, Australia
(a division of Pearson Australia Group Pty. Ltd.)
Penguin Books India Pvt. Ltd., 11 Community Centre, Panchsheel Park, New Delhi—110 017, India
Penguin Group (NZ), 67 Apollo Drive, Rosedale, North Shore 0632, New Zealand
(a division of Pearson New Zealand Ltd.)
Penguin Books (South Africa) (Pty.) Ltd., 24 Sturdee Avenue, Rosebank, Johannesburg 2196,
South Africa
Penguin Books Ltd., Registered Offices: 80 Strand, London WC2R 0RL, England

Copyright © 2005 by Yvonne Sanders-Butler
Text design by Liz Sheehan
Cover design by Wendy Bass
Cover photography by www.edubphoto.com

First edition: September 2005

Library of Congress Cataloging-in-Publication Data

Sanders-Butler, Yvonne.
   Healthy kids, smart kids : why eating right makes kids bright / Yvonne Sanders-Butler with Barbara
Alpert.
      p. cm.
   "The principal-created parent-tested, children-approved program for learning better and staying
healthy for a lifetime."
   ISBN 978-0-399-53166-8
   1. Children—Nutrition—Popular works. 2. School children—Nutrition—Popular works. I. Alpert,
Barbara. II. Title.
   RJ206.S235 2005

PRINTED IN THE UNITED STATES OF AMERICA

10 9 8 7 6 5 4 3 2

To my childhood friend, "Charlie," who did not survive his own struggle with obesity and overeating. It was you, Charlie, whom I thought of when I created the Sugar-Free Zone at my school, and it is your smile, Charlie, that I see when I watch children running, playing, and eating healthier. We did it, Charlie! We started a Wellness Revolution!

Table of Contents

Table of Contents

Introduction

Seeing the Problem,
Finding the Solution

_____

I spend every day of my working life with children. As an elementary school principal, I take responsibility for hundreds of children each morning, and when I return them to their families each afternoon, I do it with the hope and expectation that they will have been safe and well cared for.

But I'm also a parent, and I know firsthand that raising healthy children takes a deep commitment and a willingness to make unpopular decisions sometimes. That means saying "no" when our children want something we believe will hurt them—physically, emotionally, psychologically, or spiritually. That means remembering that we're the adults, and that it's up to us to model for our children the kind of healthy choices we hope they will make for the rest of their lives.

An important part of my job is observation. Each day I must be aware of how well my staff runs Browns Mill School and where there are problems or challenges that require my involvement. I need to evaluate my teachers to be sure they're successful in engaging their students and getting their lessons across; I have to study the assessments we give our children to decide if we need to change what we're doing to ensure they are learning to the best of their abilities.

As the leader of my school, I also have to consider the well-being of my students and staff. That can be as simple as arranging for necessary building repairs, and as complex as devising a program to help our kids reclaim their physical health.

I certainly wasn't the first person to notice that far too many of our nation's students are suffering the effects of a poor diet and inadequate physical activity. You can't pick up a newspaper or turn on the evening news without reading or hearing about the obesity epidemic that is plaguing the people of our wealthy and powerful country.

But the news is worse than it used to be because this health crisis has begun affecting the millions of younger Americans—the children of school age. As more of our children get fewer periods of physical education each week, as fast food and soda vending machines find a home in our schools, as video games and computer time replace the traditional energetic play of childhood, we are at a crossroads, and the lives of our children are at stake.

This book is the culmination of a dream I had to transform the lives of the children in my care, but I also wrote it to help all those other kids—those whose families love them dearly but may not have figured out how to help them achieve academic success and optimum health with a program of lifestyle changes that the whole family can use.

Much of what you're about to read is good old-fashioned common sense, updated with the latest nutrition research and presented in language that you can use to transform your life and the lives of your children. In these pages, you'll discover what's endangering our kids, how to make changes that you all can live with, and why you need to start *now* to get your family on the right track! Reading between the lines, you'll also find my passionate desire to give all of our children an equal chance to live long, healthy lives and find the energy to fulfill their dreams.

There's no time to lose! Your children grow and change every single day, and every day you've got an opportunity to guide and encourage them to be the best they can be.

Leading by Example

My Own Story

When I push my cart through our local super-market, I sometimes experience a kind of sensory overload. There are so many products with so many different health claims, it's not surprising that parents everywhere find shopping such an exhausting and confusing chore.

I used to have a very different experience when I set out to buy groceries. Everywhere I looked, I saw sweets—candies, cookies, cakes, frozen treats, sweet breads, and sweet cereals—and I wanted to eat them all.

So I did. I was a busy working parent who was also going to graduate school, and I told myself I needed the energy, the boost that sugar always gave me. I didn't pay any attention to the voice inside reminding me that every sugar "high" was followed by a crash, when I lost focus and became lethargic and sluggish. The only solution I knew was to eat something, and most of the time what I ate was high in calories, sugar, and fat.

The result of these behaviors wasn't surprising: I was over-weight, I was moving rapidly toward developing type 2 diabetes, and my blood pressure was edging toward the kind of numbers that my doctor had warned me against. But was I listening to those warnings? Or did I need a more "eye-opening" wake-up call?

I guess I did, because I got one.

One evening in 1996, I'd shared a wonderful meal with friends and family, celebrating my acceptance into the doctoral program at the University of Sarasota. After years of hard work, during which I'd risen from teacher's aide to certified teacher, been a counselor and administrator, and was now an assistant principal (before I moved to Browns Mill as principal), I was excited by the opportunity to study for my doctorate.

But by 1 AM, I had to be rushed to the hospital. One of my eyes was inexplicably swollen and red, my heart was pounding a mile a minute, and my blood pressure had risen to 200/140.

When the emergency room doctors told me that I was on the verge of having a stroke, I felt shocked, guilty, and scared.

Shocked, because I couldn't believe this was happening to a woman still in her thirties. A stroke? Wasn't that something that only happened to old people with weak hearts and hardened arteries?

Guilty, because years earlier I'd been diagnosed with sarcoidosis, an inflammatory disease with arthritis-like symptoms. When my then-doctor told me that I needed to lose weight, lower the stress in my life, and eat a healthy, balanced diet, I'd shaken my head and laughed. I was a veteran dieter, and I knew that this was one prescription I was unlikely to follow.

Scared, because I wanted to live. I had so much to live for, and so much I still wanted to accomplish. My ears were wide open, and I was finally ready to hear the message I'd ignored for so many years. I knew I was smart enough to make the changes that would give me a second chance at life. You see, I'd already come so far.

I've heard it said that a near-death experience is a great

teacher. It reminds you that your time on this earth is limited, and that things will never be exactly the same again. At least they won't be if you want to live a long life.

After my health scare, I got serious. I joined an overeating support group and I didn't just sit and listen; I participated. I began doing serious research into the facts about eating for health, and I stopped being seduced by the latest best-selling diet books based on nutrition fads. I recognized that I was the only person who could make the necessary changes in my life. No one could drag me off my unhealthy path and make me walk the "straight and narrow." It was up to me to choose to get better, to be better, and to live a life inspired by better choices.

Some of us take years before we learn these lessons, and some, sadly, never learn them. I've attended way too many funerals for people I loved, people who lost their lives too young because they succumbed to serious health problems.

In the Beginning

I started out life as the sixth of eight children, the daughter of sharecroppers in rural Mississippi. I'd learned early that food, any food, on the table was a blessing, and that cooking well for your loved ones was a gift, a way to show your love. My mother shared all her cooking and baking secrets with me, and I even earned a nickname, Sugarwoman, because of my love of sweets.

But though I adored desserts, I grew up eating a healthier diet than many impoverished people do today. Why? As sharecroppers' children, we ate off the land, so our daily diet consisted of fruits and vegetables we could raise ourselves or trade for with our neighbors, along with small amounts of meat and poultry raised by our parents or by others in our small community.

We rarely if ever ate at fast-food restaurants or were treated to deep-fried foods; we just didn't have access to them. Homemade sweets—pies, cakes, cookies, even ice cream cranked in an old-fashioned freezer—were all we ever saw, and even those were special occasion foods, not something we got every day.

Still, there was no denying that I was powerfully affected by sugar, even from a young age. When I was in second grade, I had my first taste of chocolate milk. Most children try it, and nothing of note occurs. But for me it was the start of something more than a little dangerous. That day, I ate my lunch with friends at the three-room school I attended in my rural Mississippi town. I finished lunch with a big cookie and the chocolate milk.

Next thing I knew, it was as if I'd been injected with adrenaline! I had all kinds of energy that would not allow me to sit still or think straight. I became anxious, too, enough so that my teacher noticed and allowed me to go outside and run around to burn off all that extra energy the sweets had given me. I've seen that same reaction in many children over the years, especially after they've consumed party treats like cupcakes or sugary soda or finished lunch with cookies and chocolate milk.

Once I left home, and that simpler, healthier way of life, to pursue my education, my eating habits changed for the worse. Suddenly I was faced with a much wider variety of foods to choose from, and many of those foods were as high in fat and sugar as they were irresistible to a young woman who'd grown up in a rural area and rarely enjoyed such a rich diet.

As an inevitable result, I gained much more than the "freshman fifteen" pounds, and I kept putting on weight as I ate what I loved, without giving much thought to the health dangers of what I was consuming.

Just as many of us do, I gained weight, then dieted much of the excess off, then went back to eating just as I liked. The cycle would continue year after year, as new diets sounded like the perfect solution to my eating problems, for as long as they lasted! I was a textbook yo-yo dieter—up and down, up and down, year after year.

I didn't know then (and might not have done things any differently, anyway) that this kind of constant gaining and losing weight was dangerous; I don't think I realized that I was stressing my heart, putting my body through the wringer, and sacrificing my good health in the name of eating the foods I loved.

I was lucky—I got a warning in time to do something about it, and I found the strength to make the lifestyle changes that I'm convinced saved my life. But even as I feel grateful for my own second chance, I think of my childhood friend, whom we affectionately called Charlie Brown, who didn't survive his own struggle with obesity and overeating.

In the past twenty years, researchers tell us, the number of overweight and obese youth has doubled, but even as we shake our heads at this disturbing statistic, we still manage to push it to the backs of our minds. It's only when we can put a face on the problem that it becomes truly real to us. So even as I work to change the lives of my students and their families, I think of Charlie, my kindergarten sweetheart, who loved sweets as much as he loved me, but whose unhealthy eating habits ultimately cost him his life and left me without the support of his lifelong friendship.

When we were just kids, Charlie began looking out for me, breaking the rules to let me play marbles with the neighborhood boys. As we grew older, we remained dear friends and confidants, even as we shared a passion for living and a deep understanding of each other's needs.

We also shared a long-term struggle with our weight. But while

I was able to make the changes that finally helped me lose my own extra pounds, Charlie was not. He had become morbidly obese in the last few years of his life, and while he managed to lose more than 150 pounds in the months before he died, it was not enough to keep him alive. At the time he died, due to complications from surgery, Charlie weighed more than four hundred pounds and suffered from a number of serious health problems.

His spirit and love of life endures in me, encouraging me never to give up the struggle. His legacy is the renewed lives of the many children and adults who have been, and continue to be, helped by the principles of sugar-free healthy living.

It was Charlie I thought of back in 1998, when I first noticed an overweight boy, one of my students, trading away the last of his prized baseball cards for a friend's french fries and brownie. I felt a physical ache at the notion of a child's surrendering something he loved for the momentary pleasure of a high-fat, high-sugar meal. I knew that once he had devoured the fries and brownie, he would become depressed at having lost his cards, and that sadness would likely lead to further overeating as he tried to numb himself with food.

Charlie helped to inspire the creation of the Sugar-Free Zone at my school, and his memory continues to be a force for positive change. I can visualize him smiling when I watch our kids participating in sports and making healthy choices in the cafeteria. And when I'm working late on new ways to extend the benefits of my Sugar-Free Zone Program beyond Browns Mill School, I think of Charlie—and I know he would approve.

Starting a Revolution

How We Transformed
a School and a Community

Recently I logged on to the Internet and typed a request for a definition. I was curious to see what result it would produce. The word I searched for was *revolution*—a word I've been using to describe events at the school where I serve as principal. The first answer returned, courtesy of Princeton University's Web site, seemed exactly right: "a drastic and far-reaching change in ways of thinking and behaving."

That's it. That's what I have been working toward, and that's what I want to share with you in this book. It may sound drastic, but I believe that nothing will do short of a real revolution in belief about how we nourish our children.

When I first arrived at Browns Mill School in 1998, I had a lot to learn about the community and the culture. But I immediately developed an impression of the school and of the 780 students who came through its doors each morning.

I'd been hired as the assistant principal, but within three weeks I was promoted to principal, with the enormous responsibility of directing the lives of my staff and students. Because I hadn't had time to create my own plan, I settled for running fast and hard and working with the people and programs already in place. It wasn't until a month or more into the year that I began to evaluate what we were doing, and to imagine what I'd like to see change.

Browns Mill School serves children from mostly middle-class families. It is a public school devoted to the arts and dedicated to high achievement. As I observed what was in place when I arrived, I knew it was vital to understand the system before seeking to change it. After all, as the saying goes, "If it isn't broken, don't fix it."

Before long, I became concerned about the many referrals to the school health care worker early in the day, usually before 9 AM. I noticed that a number of children appeared sluggish and complained of headaches and stomach ailments. When I asked them, "Did you eat breakfast?" too often the answer was "no."

What could I do about that? Without a decent breakfast, I knew that our children couldn't function at their best in the classroom. Research has shown that chronic or transient hunger affects up to 50 percent of all American schoolchildren, from all socioeconomic groups, which can have a devastating effect on their ability to learn.

It may sound like a cliché to say that breakfast is the most important meal of the day, but it's true: eating a healthy breakfast prepares the brain for its best work. When breakfast is skipped or consists of junk food, students may experience reading difficulties usually due to lack of concentration, irritability, and other behavioral problems. Additional research suggests that what a child eats for breakfast also has a great impact on development—physical, neurological, even emotional.

I also noticed that there were many counseling and discipline referrals directly *after* meals, which indicated to me that what my students were eating might be contributing to this problem. Many of

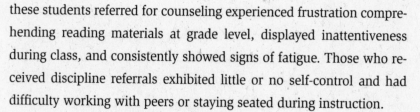

these students referred for counseling experienced frustration comprehending reading materials at grade level, displayed inattentiveness during class, and consistently showed signs of fatigue. Those who received discipline referrals exhibited little or no self-control and had difficulty working with peers or staying seated during instruction.

Were these behavior problems directly linked to what they were consuming at breakfast and lunch? I became more and more convinced that they were.

Around the same time, I became aware of the number of overweight children in the school. It appeared that as the number of students with weight concerns was ballooning upward, younger students were going on diets, either choosing on their own to limit their food intake because they felt fat or getting a strong message from family members that they needed to lose weight.

I knew the problem wasn't unique to my school. I'd read that students across the country were starting to diet at an earlier age than they used to but weren't getting results. In a recent study, more than half of fourth graders described themselves as "on a diet," compared to a time twenty-five years earlier when you didn't see this kind of behavior until the children reached age thirteen.

I started to watch carefully what the children brought to school for lunch. I took note that the cafeteria regularly served french fries, pizza, macaroni and cheese, and fried chicken. Who was eating what? About 40 percent of our students receive a subsidized free lunch; another 20 percent bring their lunches from home, and the remaining 40 percent purchase their lunches at school. What else were they consuming during lunch periods? I needed to know more. I learned that most kids drank chocolate milk and gobbled down sweet desserts, often while leaving most of the entrée on their trays.

I began to see the outlines of the problem. But it got worse: I noticed that some children traded food off their trays to collect extras of their favorites. One child might end up with three or four chocolate milks, while few of the children were eating any vegetables, even as USDA regulations were written to increase the vegetable content in school lunches (and to stop counting ketchup as a vegetable, as they did not so long ago!). We also had the problem of little kids being coerced by older students to give up their sweets and treats.

After these high-fat, high-calorie, high-sugar lunches, at least a third of the kids would go back to their classrooms and fall asleep. Or they'd become hyperactive and start "bouncing off the walls," disrupting or annoying the rest of the class.

I needed my students to get and stay focused. How? By making sweeping changes in how we fed our kids.

First Steps

Once I decided that I had to take action to provide my students with better nutrition to support their academic and physical well-being, I formed a nutritional leadership team, which consisted of representatives from all those who held a stake in the students' success: the cafeteria manager, three teachers, our head custodian, a bus driver, three parents, members of the student government and the 4-H Club, and several area grocery-store managers.

I shared my concerns with the members of the team and outlined my vision for change. Our first step was to review the school's cafeteria menus, and we discovered that, while their purpose was to ensure that students received the basic daily nutrients, little attention was paid to the amount of hidden sugars, salt, and other "culprits" that these meals contained.

Eventually, we came up with the following recommendations:

• To create a team that included the cafeteria manager, staff members, and myself that would be responsible for reviewing and selecting all of the scheduled meals that would be served.

• To eliminate refined sugar, high fat, and processed foods and drinks from the school menu.

• To provide more fresh vegetables, salads, fruits, and natural snack treats on the school menu.

• To make only water and 100 percent fruit juices available at the school.

• To replace all sugary sodas with bottled water in the school vending machines.

• To design menus to support students and staff members with special dietary needs, such as those with diabetes, high blood pressure, and high cholesterol.

Once our criteria were established, we set ourselves a goal to start the program in the fall of 1999 and create the first sugar-free school environment in the United States. Pretty ambitious!

But even with such a dedicated team, we couldn't do this on our own. We needed the full support and participation of teachers, staff, parents, the community, and, most important, the students.

The Teachers and the Staff

From the bus drivers who carry the students to school each day; to the cafeteria workers preparing and serving breakfast, lunch, and snacks; to the teachers—regardless of their subject—each person who comes in contact with children has an opportunity to make their lives better.

The bus drivers for Browns Mill have been given the authority to "confiscate" candy or other high-sugar, high-fat foods from any child on their buses. These items are placed in a bag and given to the assistant principal along with a note. The assistant principal then calls the parents to remind them of our rules and decides if the confiscated items should be disposed of or given to the parent. Most times the candy ends up in the trash.

If a teacher or other member of the staff observes a child eating any "empty calorie" food in the school, the same procedure applies.

But taking on the role as food police is only one small part that the school staff plays in our campaign to get healthy. Before the school term begins, we provide training and support to help teachers get the message across to the children because it's vital that they "model" this new behavior for the students. And that means not drinking sugary sodas or eating candy bars when they are in the public areas of the school.

When we first started, most teachers bought into the program right away. For others, it wasn't so easy because many of them had the same kinds of unhealthy eating habits as their students and were pretty resistant to making changes.

I appealed to their hearts as much as to their stomachs: "Please do it even if *you* don't want to, because our children's lives are at stake." I added that I was confident they would see the benefits quickly both in terms of behavioral issues and academic achievement, which was bound to reflect well on them.

They recognized the teaching potential in the program, too. Nutrition is an ideal subject for cross-curricular study, whether kids were learning to read food labels (literacy), calculating how many servings in a package (math), or learning about how the body metabolizes the foods we eat to give us energy (science).

We teach our kids the facts so they will be smart consumers of health information. There is just so much out there, especially now with the Internet, and we talk to the children about why it's important to consider the source of all information, not just that on health and nutrition, and to read critically.

We explain how diabetes develops, how the arteries harden when we eat too much fat and cholesterol, and how easy it is to become overweight if you eat more than you burn. And we demonstrate all the many fun ways to burn calories by activity. They learn there are no quick fixes, but a commitment to a healthy life can be lasting.

We also teach the children to read labels carefully, to understand what the numbers really mean, and to select from different food groups in the course of a day. It's part of our Quality Core Curriculum, along with teaching our children the ways to succeed in the world through manners and etiquette. Right from the beginning, we explain the rules and regulations along with acceptable behavior and provide a nutrition orientation and a clear list of what they can and cannot bring to school. We invite the kids to ask a lot of questions, and they do. And we provide our teachers with age-appropriate K–6 lesson plans to make the curriculum stick.

One of our kindergarten teachers launched a health and nutrition lesson by inviting children to identify all the foods that are in the fruit group. After listing student ideas on chart paper, the teacher assigned the children to make a collage that included as many fruits as possible. For those following her example, there are several ways to do this: cut photos from magazines, use a photocopied handout of fruit pictures that the children color first and then cut out, or even set up a buffet of real fruit for the children to draw, paint, or sketch. A field trip to a local farmers' market also provides a vivid, multisensory experience for the students, allowing them to look, touch, taste, smell, and even listen—the crunch of a Red Delicious apple or the snap of a fresh piece of celery will remind them of the wonders of fresh food.

· First graders learned to keep a Healthy Fruit Journal in which they wrote the names of each fruit they consumed during a given day, with the suggestion that they try to eat at least three pieces each day for a week. They also drew smiley faces next to healthy food choices (carrot, apple, bread, skim milk) and frowning faces next to unhealthy ones (potato chips, chocolate).

Another age-appropriate learning activity that's fun but also delivers educational value is the Healthy Food Grab Bag, with which students use their sense of touch to identify foods and then decide whether a food is healthy or unhealthy. Foods to hide in the bag might include an orange, a slice of bread, a banana, grains of rice, a tomato, or cornflakes.

Without looking inside the bag, they must decide the following:

- How hard or soft is it?
- How is it shaped?
- What kind of texture can I feel when I hold it?
- What do I know about this food so I can decide if it is good for me or not?

The teachers also introduced important vocabulary words: *nutritious*, *protein*, *carbohydrates*, *fats*, *fiber*, and *calories*, just for a start.

And once Browns Mill became a Sugar-Free Zone, the teachers stopped giving candy as a reward. We found that we could use non-food treats—special pencils, erasers, bookmarks, posters, even glowin-the-dark snakes for special science standouts—with equal effect. And these goodies lasted much longer than a lollipop.

The Changes That Began in the Kitchen

It's not an easy thing to persuade Southern cooks to change the way they do things. In the South, more is better—more butter, more sugar, more of everything.

I couldn't just order the cooks to help us change the way the school ate. I had to get them to *want* to help, and so I shared my own story with them. "I almost died, but God gave me a second chance, so I'm going to use it. You have kids and grandkids, and some of what's going to happen to these kids starts here in this kitchen." I think my sincerity won them over. But by asking for their help on behalf of the children, I empowered them to take the initiative, to actively join in the battle.

First we went after sugar and high-carbohydrate junk foods, which I called "the Enemy." We knew that kids fought over these unhealthy "treats." Some would even lie or steal to get them. When we served pancakes, some children would stockpile five or six packets of syrup! We didn't take away everything sweet, of course. We still serve cling peaches in their own juices (this is Georgia, after all!) and Jell-O. But eliminating unhealthy sweets takes vigilance and a willingness to stand firm.

Finding Students to Lead the Way

I wanted to start generating support among the student body with a select team who would spread the word. I decided to appeal to their pride and competitive nature. I believed they would do whatever it took to beat their competitors, even if it meant giving up a little sugar.

I began with the Browns Mill student leaders. Our student council members had been elected by their peers, and they were indeed a strong group of young people whom the entire student body admired. I met with them and invited them to taste some of my new recipes, later named Mom's Choice because of their kid appeal! I was confident that they would like them, but even I was surprised by their enthusiasm.

After the students sampled the recipes, I asked them to be honest and tell me what they thought. You can count on one thing: children at this age will almost always be brutally honest with you, but that's what I needed. They genuinely liked what they tasted. Several even suggested ways to make certain recipes better, and they were right!

Now that I had sparked their interest, I shared with the students how proud I was of them and how special I thought they each were. I added that one of the main goals of the student government was to create good programs for our school, and I noted my concern about the connection between academic achievement and their health.

I asked if they knew anyone who had diabetes, hypertension, or cancer, or anyone who was overweight. All of their hands flew up immediately. Some even said they had known some relatives who had died recently because of some of those diseases. I knew I had their attention.

"You all are destined to do great things," I told them, "but in order to be all you want to be, you've got to stay healthy and help your friends and families stay healthy, too." My brightest and youngest asked what it would take to make this happen at Browns Mill.

"Hard work," I answered, "and you can do it." I informed them that most of the Browns Mill students were not achieving at the level that I knew they were capable of, and I suggested that I might know the reason. I asked them how many ate fruits and vegetables each day, and how many drank five or more glasses of water a day. Only a small number of the group raised their hands. "Why do you think fruits, vegetables, and water will make a difference in your success?" They figured it out quickly, and the questions began to fly.

One student said, "Eating like this, it's as if we are dying a slow death, aren't we?"

"Well, we are certainly not extending our lives," I responded, "but we can choose to change all that."

The school leaders realized that the success of this program would depend largely on them. They didn't all buy into it right away, but I think they knew they had a job to do and I believed that they would do it, no matter what. I asked them to suggest the best way to share what we'd been talking about with the rest of the student body. "Give classes about healthy living," one child offered. "Start keeping a journal to log what you eat and how much water you drink." I said we'd do all that and more. I announced that I was creating a cooking club for students and invited them to be its first members. "Bring your parents," I added. I explained that during our club meetings twice a month we would prepare healthy meals and treats that would be easy to try at home.

That's how we began, and it grew from there. An incredible journey so far, it's been "by the kids, for the kids, and with the kids" that we made it happen. From the first time I spoke to the students, I told them it would be the children who ensured the success of the Sugar-Free Zone Program at Browns Mill. Empowered from the beginning, they knew that what they thought and said mattered. They could have great test scores, they could improve their own lives, *and* they could save the health of all the people they loved.

Partnering with Parents

I knew that to be successful we had to get parents to buy into the Sugar-Free Zone Program, and I remember telling myself that the positives of the program I was proposing must outweigh the negatives by far. So what could I tell the parents that would make them, and their children, be willing to give up that favorite food of all time—sugar?

I already knew that Browns Mill was not a community to which one could *dictate* anything. These parents had money, education, and clout. It was a middle-class to upper-middle-class community, where more than 50 percent of the adults had college degrees and more than 60 percent had well-paying jobs. I knew that about 90 percent of them believed that Browns Mill was a good school, one that would afford their children many opportunities to be successful. We had a strong Parent-Teacher Association (PTA) that kept its finger on the pulse of the curriculum and cared about the achievement of the children. They were always looking at ways that their children could do more and achieve better. I knew for sure that the parents were convinced I cared deeply about their children and wanted the best for them. But with a demanding program like the one I had in mind, would that be enough?

So I started the campaign with the PTA, and shared with them my own experiences. Equally important, I talked with them about myself as a parent and about what meant the most to me when my own son entered elementary school. I wanted him in an environment that was safe, was respected academically, and ensured that my son would get a sound educational foundation. I also wanted to find a place where I believed that the leader of the school had my son's best interests at heart and would support me in keeping him healthy and on task. I knew this would not be easy. My son, Denard, had asthma as a child, and much of the medicine used to treat his condition caused him to be hyper and off task during much of class time. He needed a school that would offer him structure, a healthy diet, and a lot of patience.

As I got ready for the next PTA board meeting, I prepared several of my favorite healthy cookie and muffin recipes. The parents really enjoyed the opportunity to taste the cookies and harvest muffins. Many commented that they were trying to watch their weight because of what they were hearing from their own doctors about health issues and weight. They were delighted to know that enjoying my treats didn't mean they were overindulging. I assured them that even these treats could be part of a healthy diet, if eaten in moderation.

The first item on the agenda was student achievement and how Browns Mill compared to other schools in the region. We planned to discuss how our students could achieve stronger academic scores and stay better focused. I announced that many of the schools in our district were as strong as we were academically, even though they had more social and academic challenges to deal with than we did. Many of these area schools, I continued, had posted test scores similar to ours.

The parents were all puzzled by this. I informed them that "more sometimes means less." Since most of our children lived socially and economically stable lives, they didn't have to come to school hungry or undernourished for lack of money to buy food. But many of the students ate regularly at fast-food joints and local restaurants, and they could purchase whatever snacks and treats they liked best at the grocery store. But they were buying empty calories!

I shared my observations about how I thought this kind of lifestyle was affecting our students. I believed that the times of day we saw many students for counseling and discipline referrals were in direct correlation with breakfast and lunch. Noting that breakfast was the most important meal of the day, I told the parents that about 20 percent of our children did not eat breakfast. Or, if they ate at home, they were devouring an overload of simple carbohydrates for breakfast—white bread, muffins, doughnuts—which regularly caused them to be off task or inattentive.

Finally, I told them about our school's rising percentages of overweight students, of children with diabetes, and of children with asthma. It wasn't just us, I added. In many ways, our school was a microcosm of what was occurring all across the country.

The Parents' Reaction

Many of the PTA board members were shocked by my report and somewhat overwhelmed by the information I'd given them. But they were eager to find out what they could do to improve their children's health and increase test scores.

"You must serve and support the whole child," I said. "A fragmented approach gives you fragmented results." I added that in my role as an administrator, I felt an enormous responsibility to my students. Their success would be my success, and I wanted to take a newly holistic approach, what I believed to be a "bulletproof formula" for a program of rigorous academics that was solidly supported by nutrition and physical fitness. I saw them nodding at what I said, but I felt that I needed to go further to win their complete support.

I appealed to them directly by sharing my personal life struggle, how I felt that I had been given a second chance to touch lives in a way that could make a significant difference. I said that I not only wanted the best for their children academically, but I wanted them to live long enough to achieve all their hopes and dreams, whatever they might be. If we didn't intervene now, too many of our children might suffer so many health problems by young adulthood that they will not be able to reach those heartfelt goals.

I believed that most of the parents saw the value in the nutrition and physical fitness program I was proposing, but I could still see hesitation in many of their faces. I was stumped by this. Was their hesitation due to the fact that for much of the past decade, parents seemed more concerned about what pleased their children than what was best for them? Sometimes I wasn't sure who ran the household!

The more information we could make available to our families, the better they would accept and support the school's efforts. We provided a list of Web sites and other resources so they would be able to make similar changes at home, as well as to provide the ingredients for healthy lunches and snacks if they wanted their children to bring their own.

From the very beginning, I made regular communication with our families an integral part of the plan. We sent biweekly newsletters home, selecting a "health focus" for each month—diabetes, hypertension, exercise. We highlighted what the children were learning about nutrition and tied it into whatever home and community celebrations were part of that monthly calendar. One month we included a report headlined "Hydrate the Brain!" on the importance of getting enough water into our bodies each day.

Immediately, parents stepped up and arranged for hundreds of bottles of water to be donated to the school, which was a tremendous reminder that the community is often eager to support a school's efforts. You just have to take the initiative and ask. Over the years, our parents had arranged generous donations for our special events, such as hundreds of ice cream cups for a field day picnic.

Now we needed them to understand that we still wanted their help, but we had to see healthier choices in what we were offering the children. We also encourage our parents to volunteer to work at the school, not only to support academic or extracurricular activities but to support our nutritional program.

> I have come a long way! As a former advocate of sweets, I was terrified when I heard about the Sugar-Free Program at my daughter's school. It was too close for comfort. I respected you for your accomplishments as an educator but I was scared beyond belief that you would make me confront some of my own demons.
>
> I know I was probably one of your most difficult parents and did not appreciate what you were trying to do for our children. I know that I talked down about the program and you taking your authority to the limit.
>
> I am a single parent and my load is very heavy. However, it is lighter in weight for me and I am not miserable anymore. My daughter loves the program. We spread the word wherever we go. Oh! Did I tell you that I have a personal trainer now?
>
> —Browns Mill School parent

It Takes a Village . . .

The bounds of influence of staff, teachers, and parents are limited, and I knew that "out there," between the school gate and the front door, were lots of temptations for even the most motivated child.

I talked to the "candy lady," who sold goodies to the kids after school. I didn't want to take away part of her livelihood, but she understood what we were trying to do at the school, and now she no longer markets sweets to children near our building.

Even though I had invited several supermarket managers to be part of my initial team to get the Sugar-Free Program going, once school was in session, I asked each class to create a list of favorite foods that they believed to be healthy. Then, with my own lists and those the children provided, I set out to visit all of the grocery-store managers in our community to share my plan and to solicit their support to help my program be a success. They were all very accommodating.

As weeks and months went by, I saw more of the foods we requested on the store shelves. I saw more shelf space being designated to items that used to be called "health nut" foods. I also saw special incentives offered by some stores to increase parent awareness of what they now stocked. Stores scheduled taste-testing events to advertise the arrival of new healthy products. They also provided generous donations of fruit and healthy snacks for our parties, field days, Arts Galas, and Olympic activities.

SUGAR ANONYMOUS

I had been a member of OA (Overeaters Anonymous) for several years when I first launched the program at Browns Mill. I decided to begin a healthy living support group at the school. I opened it up to parents, teachers, bus drivers, anyone in the community who wanted to join us. I invited people of all ages to come and learn how to create a balanced lifestyle with nutrition and exercise.

I named my group SA—for Sugar Anonymous. In this class, we took field trips to the grocery store and farmers' markets to show families how to shop and get the best bargains. I also brought in unfamiliar foods and ingredients that would be helpful in structuring their new food plan—items like soy milk, unbleached flours, wheat and oat flours, soy margarines, and more. I started a bimonthly cooking class for parents to demonstrate how easy it was to prepare healthy recipes, appealing especially to the people who voiced that cooking this way would be too difficult or expensive. I showed them how simple it was to modify family favorites and how tasty these recipes could be. Our monthly sessions covered topics ranging from "How to Shop for Your Family" to "Preparing Healthy Meals and Snacks on Short Notice."

Learning by Doing

3

A Curriculum for
Teaching Nutrition to Kids
and Adults

Browns Mill has become an exciting laboratory to help us understand and help our students. We're doing a body mass index (BMI) study on our fourth graders and issuing them pedometers, so they can keep a journal and chart of their daily activity. It's a great cross-curricular activity—writing and math combined!

I believe this program works because it takes a positive focus. It also requires a strong will and a genuine commitment to change. But once you know the facts, and I share those with even our youngest students, it's hard not to take action.

There's a lot to be said for boosting a child's positive attitude through this program. When kids feel good about themselves, they do better; research has proved it. I know the power an educator has to make a difference in children's lives, so I'm determined to use my clout and my energy to, as I say in my opening speech to the students, "make you the brightest, smartest kids who can do anything!"

I am sugar-free because sugar can make you have rotten teeth, and too much sugar can make you sick. I quit sugar everywhere. I quit sugar by staying away from it. Most people like sugar, like me, but I'm trying to stay away from it. If you like sugar, you can try what I did. You can still have fun without candy, trust me. I know, and I know because I have been through it.

—Jenee, second grade

Making the Program Work

I was both inspired and excited by the opportunity to institute a program at my school that I believed would change so many lives for the better. I knew it wouldn't be easy, but I was in it for the long haul and prepared to use all my energy and gift for persuasion to get everyone—parents, children, community—on board!

We began the year with an open house for families so that I could present a compelling overview of the Sugar-Free Program to them. As I explained what our team had planned in the coming months, I advised the parents that they would need to play a vital role in helping to implement the new nutritional program if it were to be successful. I described how it all could work:

• Parents can ensure that their children eat well by preselecting their meals from the menus that the school sends out each month. If parents opt to have their children bring their lunches to school, parents need to ensure that the lunches are nutritionally sound according to the government's food pyramid and the nutritional food list that the school provides.

• If items like cookies, candies, soda, and similar foods are included in lunches brought from home, these "not-recommended" items will be collected from the child and an appropriate substitute will be provided by the school in exchange for the items.

- The bus drivers are not only responsible for delivering the children safely to school and home again but also for ensuring that unhealthy snacks are not eaten on the bus.

- The grocery-store managers agree to ensure that the foods families need to take care of their health will be in stock.

- Teachers and parents can stay in closer touch than ever through an expanded school newsletter that will deliver information about the nutrition program and suggest ways to support the school's efforts at home.

Once we got the program started, we knew we had to keep interest high and continue to provide encouragement and resources to our families. As the year progressed, I met on a monthly basis with our nutrition team and the PTA to maintain support and continue to educate parents about the potential problems that bad eating habits could produce. Students received and discussed the school "nutritional contract" in their classrooms; it was then sent home for parents to review with their child before signing and returning it to the child's homeroom teacher.

The Commitment Contract

I asked every child and parent in my school to sign a "commitment contract" as part of our program. Why? There's just something about putting your name on paper that helps even the youngest children realize they're making a serious promise.

Our "Achieving Academic Excellence through Nutrition" commitment contract had two versions and six parts: for our preschool through second-grade children, aged four to seven, the contract reads,

I PROMISE TO

- Eat a healthy breakfast each morning because it will supply the fuel I need each day to do my best work in school.
- Drink five to eight glasses of water during the day so I can help my brain, kidneys, lungs, heart, and muscles work better.
- Eat five vegetables and fruits each day that are yellow, green, red, white, and purple to help me to be strong and healthy.
- Exercise each day for at least thirty minutes, which may include dancing, swimming, walking, and singing, to keep my heart healthy.
- Go to bed early each night so that I can have a healthy body and mind for school each day.
- Avoid foods that have too much sugar, salt, and fat so that I will stay healthy and maintain a healthy weight.

For our older children, grades three to six and aged eight to eleven, the contract language is more complex, but the basic commitment is the same:

I PROMISE TO

- Eat a daily breakfast which will consist of "good" carbohydrates and proteins and which will provide the fuel I need to be productive in school.
- Drink five to eight glasses of water a day to ensure that I support the vital organs of my body (liver, kidneys, and lungs) and increase my mental functioning.
- Eat nine vegetables and fruits a day to provide the fiber, vitamins, and minerals to help me to be strong and healthy.
- Exercise each day for at least forty-five minutes, which may include dancing, swimming, walking, and running, to keep my heart healthy.

- Go to bed early each night so that I can have a healthy body and mind for school each day.
- Avoid foods that have too much sugar, salt, and fat so that I will stay healthy and maintain a healthy weight.

I asked each student *and* his or her parents and teachers to sign the pledge so that they would feel committed to the child's success and would do all they could to help. I kept the original in my files and gave a copy of the contract to everyone involved. I suggested they post it somewhere at home (the refrigerator, a family bulletin board) as a visible reminder of what to do.

And for the children who fulfilled their commitment, I awarded a special certificate at year's end during a festive ceremony in the school auditorium, with parents and other guests present. You'll surely want to make your own certificate to celebrate your family's own success on the program!

Monitoring Our Progress

We continued to consult our parents throughout the year, sending home surveys, scheduling parent-teacher meetings to share new findings about nutrition, and offering cooking workshops to build parents' confidence in cooking and eating sugar-free. I knew how convincing a cooking demo could be. Early on, when I was making my best efforts to get all of our teachers to come on board, I even cooked for the school staff to show them what I had in mind!

It didn't take long to start seeing positive results from our efforts. By the second semester of the school year, we had collected data indicating that the number of students who visited the nurse during the first hour of the school day had decreased by 30 percent. Additionally, we saw a 28 percent drop in teacher referrals for

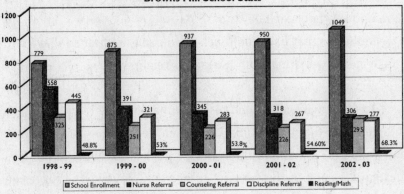

Browns Mill School Stats

Nurse Referral: Students who were seen by the nurse and a parent was contacted.

Counseling Referral: Students who were referred by teachers and parents for behavioral and emotional support. (They may be also involved in several of the support groups provided.)

Discipline Referral: Students who had problems staying on task or who exhibited inappropriate conduct such as fighting (as outlined in the *DeKalb County School Handbook*). Ten percent of all discipline concerns represent repeated violations by the same students.

Reading/Math: Percentage of students who met or exceeded grade standards.

disciplinary concerns and a 23 percent decrease in the number of students referred for counseling.

As our overweight children slimmed down and all of our students became more active, we felt a new spirit energize the entire school, and we saw evidence of the positive changes in our students' standardized test scores. This told us that the program was delivering success on all fronts!

It's great to think that as I'm writing this, Browns Mill is in the first year that every one of the students, except those newly arriving, has been part of the school as a Sugar-Free Zone.

The long-term results of this campaign for healthier eating in school continue to exceed expectations. The program proved more than successful in modifying our children's behavior, and as it goes on, we still have fewer disciplinary problems than similar schools in our region experience. Better still, we've noted fewer absences for illness. We also have no students with type 2 diabetes and only four with juvenile diabetes. Out of one thousand children, only two are being treated for hypertension. You've gotta love those numbers!

Now it's your turn. I want this book to provide you with the information you need to help your own children get healthy and improve their performance in school. There are more than 51 million elementary and secondary students in the United States, and more of them than ever before—more than 16 percent and rising—are overweight. One in four overweight children already shows early signs of type 2 diabetes; 60 percent already have one risk factor for heart disease.

But it's not too late to fix what may be "broken" when it comes to your children's nutrition and performance in school. Please, join me in a journey to better health for your entire family—and a future of excellence for every child.

> To me, to be sugar-free feels good. I have more energy now that I don't eat as much sugar as I used to. When I used to eat sugar, I felt kind of dizzy. I lost my focus. But now I have focus, I'm not dizzy, and I have energy. When you eat sugar, you will get sick. You will get your kidneys messed up. Being sugar-free is a good thing. You don't have to go to the hospital. You don't have to have surgery. If you eat sugar while you are a child, you will be fat when you are an adult.
>
> —*Carmen, second grade*

Eating for Health and Happiness

4

What We Need to Know
about What We Eat and Drink;
Special Foods and
Special Needs

Is it any wonder that so many of us have put off taking those first steps toward a healthier lifestyle? As I found with many of the teachers, staff, and parents at my school, even the brightest and best educated of us are confused about the facts of what's healthy and what's not. How could we expect our children to make the best choices for themselves? It seems that every day someone comes up with a new, surefire way to lose weight and get healthier: low-fat, low-carb, no white food, no foods with a face. Fads and fashions in nutrition appear to come and go with the seasons. There is so much conflicting information out there that it is hard to make sense of it all.

But the one thing that I've discovered is that living healthfully doesn't have to be about sacrifice or deprivation, even if your first impulse is to cut back or cut out many favorite foods. Because food is important to our mental and physical well-being, because some of the best times in our lives are built around family meals, we need to find a way to eat well and for good health *without* eliminating the pleasure we take in eating together. It is all about finding a balance that works well for you and your children.

The first step on the path to health is to become an informed consumer. Have you become an avid reader of food labels? You wouldn't dream of buying a car or a camera without checking out all the specs first to see if the product meets your needs. You might be in for a big surprise the next time you have a look at the label on one of your favorite packaged foods. What's the first ingredient? Did you check out the calories against the serving size?

We didn't develop our program for Browns Mill School without first getting a few facts straight. I am not a professional nutritionist, but as an administrator responsible for the well-being of one thousand students, I made it my business to get as much reliable information as I could. Our program, like many of the foods we recommend, is organic. It changes in response to the needs of the children and to what we might learn along the way. For instance, we paid attention when the federal government issued its new nutritional guidelines at the beginning of 2005. These recommendations are highlighted in this chapter and at the end of the book. What we had to ignore was every fad and unsubstantiated claim that came along. In other words, we had to make sense of what we were reading and use our common sense.

The Latest on Dietary Guidelines

In January 2005, the U.S. Department of Health and Human Resources issued new dietary guidelines that will be incorporated into a new food guide pyramid—or what a U.S. Department of Agriculture spokeswoman called the "food guidance system."

These guidelines will be the blueprint for all government nutrition policy, including food labeling, and for all public school lunch programs.

The nutritional component of the guidelines recommends eating more fruits and vegetables, almost twice the previously recommended amount; limiting grain-based foods but favoring whole grains; eating less meat as a source of protein by drinking low-fat milk and choosing more fish rich in omega-3 acids; and reducing the amount of sodium and added sugars. (The key recommendations appear in the appendix on page 218.)

Leslie Bonci, director of sports medicine nutrition at the University of Pittsburgh Medical Center and a spokeswoman for the American Dietetic Association, explained that the focus of the new guidelines asks people to divide their plate into quarters. One-half should be filled with fruits and vegetables, one-quarter with grains, and one-quarter with protein. "We know that people are not getting what they need," she commented. "The one-half concept is a concept that they can understand. And it's a message about more of what you can add, rather than take away," she added. "It's a positive message."

The increased focus on fruits and vegetables reflects the latest research into the benefits these foods offer toward the prevention and control of many chronic diseases. Dark green leafy vegetables are high in magnesium, which is believed to help prevent cardiovascular diseases; many fruits are high in potassium, such as bananas, cantaloupe, apricots, oranges, and orange juice, which researchers suggest helps lower high blood pressure.

These foods are also high in fiber, low in calories, and rich in vitamins A and C. Eaten in sufficient quantities to satisfy appetite and instead of more calorie-dense, less healthy foods, they are likely to help people lose weight and keep it off.

Will people accept the new recommendations and this increased emphasis on fresh produce, which may be viewed as expensive and not as filling as heartier proteins? I hope so. These new guidelines represent what I've already discovered for myself, and what I hope to share with you in this book.

Choosing the Best Ingredients

At the heart of healthy eating is choosing what to eat from the incredible variety of fresh and packaged foods available to us. Too often we select products that are too high in fat or sugar or contain additives, preservatives, and chemicals that don't do a thing to help us achieve good health.

As you contemplate the jam-packed shelves in your supermarket, it's easy to feel overwhelmed by the many choices, so let me begin your "education" by sharing with you some facts about the foods that can help you feed your family better, so you can start to feel better yourself.

• • • • • • • • • • • • • • • • • • • •

As you'll see in the recipes in chapter 6, I found a way to modify foods my family enjoyed by making important changes in the ingredients. Not every culinary experiment was a success, but I began to discover what substitutions worked and built on them. In the pages that follow, you'll learn more about what I buy to make meals at home and to serve my guests. These healthy food items, which include mostly organic ingredients and natural sweeteners, are the key to eating well while achieving and maintaining your "best of health."

• • • • • • • • • • • • • • • • • • •

Where to Find These Good-for-You Ingredients

When I first started learning about many of these food products, I had to search high and low, mostly at modest health-food stores that didn't always have everything I needed. Now many communities have healthy-food supermarkets like Whole Foods, as well as many

healthy options in traditional grocery stores and even big-box empo-
riums like Costco and Wal-mart.

If you can't find what you need where you regularly shop,
speak to the store manager. Remember, you're part of a growing
movement of parents determined to ensure their children's better
health, and your neighborhood stores will want their piece of that
business!

Buying Organic

There was a time when most grocery shoppers saw signs for organic fruits and vegetables and thought, "Hmm, grown by hippies
on communes somewhere." Organic vegetables were often much
more expensive and frequently smaller than traditionally raised produce, while organic fruits often didn't look as appealing and shiny
as the rest of the apples, pears, and plums piled high in the supermarket.

But as national concern about the health impact of pesticides
grew, so did the number of people opting to purchase organic products. At the same time, shoppers began asking, "What does it mean
that something is organically raised?" and "How do I know that
what I'm buying adheres to those regulations?"

The Farmers' Market in Berkeley, California, one of the most
prominent in the country, is a terrific source for information on
the subject. Their Web site (www.ecologycenter.org/bfm/whybuy
organic.html) reminds buyers that "organic food is good food.
Good to eat, good for the environment, good for the small-scale
farmers and farmworkers who produce it."

The U.S. Department of Agriculture estimates that at the start
of the twenty-first century, half of all domestic farm products will be
produced by only 1 percent of farms. But at the same time, the Envi-

ronmental Protection Agency (EPA) reports that commercial agriculture is responsible for 70 percent of the pollution to the country's rivers and streams caused by chemicals, erosion, and animal waste runoff. What can we, as a nation, do about that? The Berkeley site suggests that "organic farming may be one of the last ways to keep both ecosystems and rural communities healthy and alive."

Some states regulate produce labeling more actively than others. California is a good example. Since the passage of the California Organic Foods Act of 1990, produce sold in California as "organically grown" must be *registered* as organic with the California Department of Food and Agriculture. No synthetic pesticides like insecticides, herbicides, fumigants, fungicides, or miticides may have been applied in the past three years to the *land* where an organic crop is grown, a *crop* already in the field, or the *produce* after it is harvested. The law further states that "organically grown crops may not be fertilized with any synthetic fertilizers. Organically grown produce may be sprayed with various naturally occurring pest-control substances such as sulfur, copper, dolomite, Bacillius Thuringensis, and diatomaceous earth." Phew!

It's a safety issue. Growing crops without these is safer for everyone: farmers, farmworkers, the environment, and, ultimately, you the consumer.

How can you be sure that what says "Certified Organic" is actually grown using safer methods? Again, using California as an example, Certified Organic produce has to be registered with the State Department of Food and Agriculture and "certified by a third-party, non-governmental organization. The California Certified Organic Farmers (CCOF) is the major certifying organization in the state. CCOF certification and verification of the organic claim covers the crop, the land on which it is grown, the farmer and the food processor."

The rules are straightforward. A three-year land transition pe-riod is required before any crop harvested from that land can be cer-tified organic. After that, CCOF-certified operations are inspected annually. What do they check? Farming practices subject to inspec-tion include long-term soil management, buffered zones between or-ganic and conventional farms, product labeling, and record keeping. Processing inspections include review of the facility's cleanliness, pest-control methods, transportation, storage, and record keeping. You can spot products of certified CCOF growers by their green and white sunflower logos.

Many small farms don't meet all the requirements for being certified as organic, but because they use low-chemical methods, they are good sources of fresh food for your family. Some will say they use "no synthetic pesticides," which means that no pesticides or only organically approved pesticides have been used in that year. It can, however, suggest that commercial, petroleum-based fertiliz-ers have been used.

If a grower says that no synthetic pesticides have been used on trees or plants, they're saying only that organically approved pesti-cides have been used in the current year on the trees or plants which produce the crop. It may mean that herbicides or commercial fertil-izers have been used on the land. If a sign says, "No synthetic pesti-cides on fruit," it means that the fruit comes from trees that were sprayed when dormant or in bloom, but that no synthetic pesticides have ever gone on the fruit itself. (This may still mean that commer-cial fertilizers and/or herbicides have been used on the land itself.)

And if you see no signs at all, you can probably assume that the fruits or vegetables have been conventionally grown in accor-dance with U.S. Department of Agriculture and California Depart-ment of Food and Agriculture regulations.

Fruits and Vegetables

As the new dietary guidelines are announced, it's clear that all of us will be eating many more servings of fruits and vegetables. We're lucky to have an enormous number of choices in both of these important healthy food categories. Here are some good safety tips for buying, handling, and serving fresh produce.

Fruits and vegetables can pick up dust and soil as they are being harvested, handled, packed, and shipped. They may also have trace amounts of chemicals and bacteria on the outer tissues that can be removed by washing. When you're at the store, look for fresh-looking fruits and vegetables that are not bruised, moldy, shriveled, or slimy. Don't buy anything that smells bad.

Buy only what you need, enough that you will use it within a few days. Apples, potatoes, and citrus fruits can be stored longer. Handle produce gently at the store. Don't put any groceries on top of your produce, as it is easily bruised.

When you get home, put your produce away promptly. Keep most of what you buy in the crisper, which has a slightly higher humidity than the rest of the refrigerator and which is better for fruits and vegetables. Get rid of any produce that you've kept too long, especially if it is moldy or slimy. Always keep all cut fruits and vegetables covered in the refrigerator.

It's very important to wash all fruits and vegetables in clean drinking water before eating, *even if you do not plan to eat the skin*, such as with melons or oranges. In most cases, don't wash your produce until you're ready to use it. However, you *can* rinse lettuce before refrigerating to help maintain crispness. Here's a useful tip: washing produce in lukewarm water helps bring out the flavor and aroma of the fruit or vegetable you are preparing.

What about more delicate fruits? Experts say that the best

Eating in Technicolor

Nutritionists advise all of us to eat a variety of foods in vivid, living color. Not sure what those foods are? We teach our youngest students a song about "eating a rainbow," and it's clear that the "pot of gold" at the end is a lifetime of better health!

RED AND WHITE (best for healthy hearts, lowering cholesterol and blood pressure)	red peppers, red onions, red grapes, tomatoes, raspberries, strawberries, radishes, beets, rhubarb, bananas, potatoes, garlic, onions, turnips, ginger, cauliflower
YELLOW AND ORANGE (good for eye health, rich in vitamin A)	cantaloupe, papaya, corn, mango, carrots, butternut squash, yellow peppers, pumpkin, sweet potatoes, pineapple, oranges
PURPLE AND BLUE (recommended for their anti-aging qualities)	purple grapes, blueberries, plums, eggplant, purple cabbage, prunes, black currants
GREEN (linked to lowering your risk of many cancers)	broccoli, Brussels sprouts, turnips, okra, asparagus, collards, green onions, kale, mustard greens, kiwi, honeydew, pears, green apples, zucchini

method for washing ripe or fragile berry fruits like strawberries, raspberries, blackberries, and blueberries is by spraying them with a kitchen sink sprayer. Use a colander so you can carefully turn the fruit as you spray.

If you do not have a sink sprayer, place your berries and soft fruit in a wire basket or colander and then into a five- to eight-quart pot of warm water. Move the basket in and out of the water several times. Change the water until the water remains clear. It's best to do this process quickly. If fruit absorbs too much water, it will lose flavor, texture, and aroma.

Dry your fruits and vegetables with paper towels, with one major exception: greens—spinach, chard, kale, and collards—should be cooked while wet, right after you wash them.

Produce used in salads, such as lettuce, radishes, and carrots, should be washed in the coldest tap water available; for maximum crispness, try immersing your greens in a mixture of ice cubes and water about a half hour before serving.

Some other good healthy fruit and veggie tips: do not use detergents when washing fruits and vegetables. The Food and Drug Administration (FDA) has not approved these for use on food. Always peel and discard outer leaves or rinds. And scrub "hearty" vegetables such as potatoes and carrots if you want to eat the fiber and nutrient-rich skin.

EASY WAYS TO "SLIP" VEGGIES INTO FAMILY MENUS

- Add chopped spinach to lasagnas and meatloaf.
- Mix shredded carrots into tuna or chicken salads.
- Create more elaborate sandwiches by adding sprouts, cucumber slices, carrot slices, radicchio, and other unexpected vegetables.
- Try grilling portobello mushrooms, eggplant, and zucchini alongside your burgers and chicken at your next cookout.
- Fill omelets with sautéed peppers, mushrooms, and tomatoes.
- Serve healthy carrot muffins and zucchini breads for snacks.

Protein: Meat, Fish, and Poultry

You've probably read in the newspapers that many of the protein sources we've always eaten may contain substances that endanger the health of our children. Some cattle may be injected with growth hormones or given antibiotics; others may be fed grains that have been sprayed with pesticides. It's also been reported that many of the fish we eat regularly may contain high levels of mercury. And every so often we hear about salmonella as a possible danger when purchasing and eating poultry products.

So what can we do? The answer I've chosen is to purchase organically raised, grass-fed meats whenever I can, to limit the quantities of certain fish to a few servings each week or month, and to take special precautions when buying and handling poultry.

Beef

A recent article in *Mother Earth News* reported, "Grass-fed meat and dairy products have less fat and more vitamin E, betacarotene and cancer-fighting fatty acids than factory-farm products. All across the country, farmers and ranchers are returning to this ancient and healthier way of raising animals. Instead of sending them to feedlots to be fattened on grain," the article reported, "farmers are keeping animals home on the range." The article went on to note that in 1999, "Researchers discovered another health benefit of grass-fed products: They're the richest known source of another good fat called conjugated linoleic acid or CLA. CLA may be one of our most potent cancer fighters. For animals given very small amounts of CLA, a mere 1.5 percent of their total calories had a 60 percent reduction in tumor growth in a study published in *Cancer Research*. CLA may fight cancer in people as well. Recently Finnish researchers found that the more CLA in a woman's diet, the lower her risk of breast cancer. Women who consumed the most CLA had an amazing 60 percent lower risk."

Want another good reason to seek out grass-fed beef? Here goes: a six-ounce steak from a grain-fed steer has almost one hundred more calories than a six-ounce steak from a grass-fed steer, according to a report in the *Journal of Food Quality*. If you eat "a typi-cal amount of beef (66.5 pounds a year), eating grass-fed beef would save you 17,733 calories a year without requiring an ounce more of willpower. At that rate you could lose about six pounds a year."

It's true that organically raised meats cost more than what you may be used to spending, but now that you're going to be eating less meat overall, the effect on your grocery budget should be minimal. Some nutritionists suggest viewing meat as a "condiment," some-thing you add to a dish that is primarily vegetable based. This is a definite change for most Americans, but the health benefits that will follow it make it worthwhile.

Pork

We've chosen not to serve pork at our school, instead empha-sizing mostly chicken, turkey, and fish; many schools do not in-clude pork on the menu, in part because they have enrolled students whose culture or religion bans eating it. But lean pork can be a reasonable choice when eaten in moderation. Just remember to prepare it with the least amount of fat possible (e.g., no fried pork cutlets) and purchase the best-quality, organically raised meat you can find.

Fish

A joint advisory from the U.S. FDA and the U.S. EPA added tuna—America's second most popular seafood after shrimp—to its list of mercury-containing fish that should be restricted in the diets of pregnant women and young children. A separate study found un-healthy pollutants in far higher amounts in farmed salmon than in wild salmon. And still another report noted high amounts of pollu-tants in fish caught in the Great Lakes.

Mercury is a real concern for us as parents. A Harvard School of Public Health study reported in the *Journal of Pediatrics* that fetuses and young children exposed to methylmercury can suffer irreversible damage to the heart as well as permanently impaired brain growth. Now, because mercury is stored in our bodies, just as it is in those of fish, women planning to have children should also avoid high-mercury fish well before they become pregnant.

The FDA and EPA advise that young children, pregnant women, nursing mothers, and women of childbearing age not eat more than two or three meals, or twelve ounces total, of fish or shellfish a week. They also suggest they should limit high-mercury fish to one serving per week.

High mercury: Atlantic halibut, king mackerel, oysters (Gulf Coast), pike, sea bass, shark, swordfish, tilefish (golden snapper), and tuna (steaks and canned albacore).

Moderate mercury: Alaskan halibut, black cod, blue (Gulf Coast) crab, cod, Dungeness crab, Eastern oysters, mahimahi, blue mussels, pollack, tuna (canned light). (Children and pregnant or nursing women are advised to eat no more than one from this list, once a month.)

Low mercury: Anchovies, Arctic char, crawfish, Pacific flounder, herring, king crab, sand dabs, scallops, Pacific sole, tilapia, wild Alaska and Pacific salmon, farmed catfish, clams, striped bass, and sturgeon. (Children and pregnant or nursing women can safely eat these two to three times a week.)

A last piece of good fish advice: if you're in a high-risk group, don't eat the skin and fatty parts of fish, where pollutants collect. Eat your fish grilled, baked, and broiled rather than fried, to avoid added fat.

Poultry

Fresh poultry (chicken, turkey, duck, and goose) should have no detectable odor. The flesh should feel firm to the touch, and the surface should not feel slick. When you shop, look for packages that feel cool and have no tears or punctures. Remember to select your poultry just before checkout and make sure all poultry, whether raw, prepackaged, or from the deli, is refrigerated right after purchase. Prevent "cross-contamination" by keeping all fresh meats separate from other items. Put raw poultry packages inside a plastic bag so no juices will drip onto other foods.

All poultry found in retail stores is either USDA inspected for wholesomeness or inspected by the state, which has its own standards equal to the federal government. The "Passed and Inspected by USDA" seal ensures that the poultry is wholesome and free from disease. Inspection is mandatory, but grading is voluntary. Poultry is graded according to USDA regulations and standards for meatiness, appearance, and freedom from defects. Grade A chickens, the best grade, have plump, meaty bodies and clean skin, and are free of bruises, broken bones, feathers, cuts, and discoloration.

Freeze fresh poultry if you do not plan to cook it within two days after purchase. Wrap chicken parts separately in heavy-duty foil, freezer bags, or plastic wrap. Be sure to press the air out of the packages before freezing.

Always wash your hands thoroughly with hot, soapy water before preparing foods and after handling raw poultry. Don't let raw poultry or juices touch prepared foods either in the refrigerator or during preparation. Don't put cooked foods on the same plate that held raw poultry. Always wash utensils that have touched raw poultry with hot, soapy water before using them for the cooked poultry. Wash counters, cutting boards, and other surfaces that raw poultry has touched. Sanitize these surfaces with a solution of a teaspoon of chlorine bleach per quart of water before using for other foods.

Thaw uncooked poultry in the refrigerator or in cold water. NEVER thaw poultry at room temperature. For quick thawing of uncooked or cooked poultry, use the microwave. Thawing time will vary according to whether you're thawing a whole bird or parts and the number of parts frozen together. Use the defrost or medium-low setting, according to the manufacturer's directions.

Other Protein Sources

Eggs

I use organic eggs or eggs from free-range hens, which are farmed without the use of hormones and pesticides. If I want to cut down on the cholesterol in a dish like a frittata or omelet, I just eliminate some of the yolks and use more egg whites.

I also use packaged egg substitutes when feasible. And at school we often use Egg Beaters or a powdered egg white mix. For baking, however, egg substitutes will not always work. When a cake recipe requires more than four eggs, for example, egg substitutes do not yield the desired results. However, they work very well in recipes for cookies, fruit breads, and puddings. In my book, *Dessert Lovers' Choice*, I've included some baked goods that are actually eggless (and you can find many eggless recipes in other health and specialty cookbooks)—an "egg-citing" development for families with children who are allergic to eggs!

Tofu

Tofu, also known as soybean curd, is a soft, cheeselike food made by curdling fresh, hot soy milk with a coagulant. A bland product that easily absorbs the flavors of other ingredients with which it is cooked, tofu is rich in high-quality protein and B vitamins while also low in sodium. Firm tofu is dense and solid; it can be cubed and served in soups, stir fried, or grilled. Firm tofu is higher in protein, fat, and calcium than other forms of tofu. Soft tofu is good for recipes that call for blended tofu. Silken tofu is a creamy product and can be used as a replacement for sour cream in many dip recipes.

The good news is you'll probably find several kinds of tofu in your local grocery store. Some of it is shelf stable and doesn't require refrigeration; other products need to be kept cold and will be found alongside chilled dairy products. Tofu is available in several different textures and can be used in dozens of different ways. I use silken regular and low-fat tofu in my ice cream recipes.

Dairy and Nondairy Alternatives

For a long time, I had no idea I was lactose intolerant. And even once I suspected a connection between the dairy foods such as ice cream or cheese that I loved and the unpleasant bloating and stomach misery that followed, I could not imagine life without ice cream, butter, cream cheese, or milk.

Many people incorrectly believe that if their diet does not include dairy products, their bodies will not receive the required amounts of protein, vitamin D, and calcium. The problem is that many dairy foods can be high in saturated fatty acids, which doctors say increase our risk of cancer.

But there are some great dairy and nondairy alternatives. Perhaps you have tried some of these—foods such as Lactaid, rice milk, soy milk, and soy cream or butter—and decided that they didn't taste the way your favorite dairy products did. You're not alone in finding these products unfamiliar and even not as tasty, but I believe you'll find, as I did, that when I started to experiment with different brands, I found products I liked. And once I began using soy products in my recipes, I discovered I felt much better.

Since I started reading the research and using soy products, I've learned that soy may help to prevent diseases such as breast cancer, heart disease, hypertension, arthritis, diabetes, and osteoporosis. Since I suffer from several of these diseases, it made sense to incorporate soy into my daily diet, and I have seen a marked improvement. Studies also suggest that soy can be helpful in the fight against obesity.

Does this mean that everyone should give up dairy? Not at all. But many of us—and our children—may benefit from using nondairy products as part of this healthy eating plan.

Milk: If you're currently using whole milk, why not start by switching to 2 percent, with your goal eventually to feed your family either 1 percent or fat-free milk.

Organic butter: When only butter will do, in certain recipes and at the table on special occasions, you may opt for organic, unsalted, hormone-free butter from most grocery or health-food stores.

Margarine: Your best choice in margarine (if you're not opting for soy margarine, see below) is a soft, tub-packed margarine that contains less trans fat than stick margarine. Check out the discussion on trans-fatty acids in the "Fats" section further on.

Cream cheese: The cream cheeses I use at the table and in recipes allow us to continue to enjoy many favorite desserts. Since regular cream cheese contains a lot of fat and is high in calories, I use Neufchâtel cheese, a reduced-fat alternative to cream cheese, or a fat-free cream cheese. I have also tried and liked a nondairy soy cream cheese that has no dairy butterfat or cholesterol.

Soy milk: One alternative to cow's milk and higher in protein than cow's milk, this milky, iron-rich liquid is a nondairy product made by pressing ground, cooked soybeans. Soy milk is cholesterol-free and low in fat and sodium. It makes an excellent milk substitute for anyone with an allergy to milk, and you'll probably find it in your store with additional flavors such as chocolate and vanilla, with more coming as parents serve this product to their children. Although it is naturally low in calcium, this milk substitute is usually fortified with calcium. Soy milk has a tendency to curdle when mixed with acidic ingredients such as lemon juice or wine; it's intentionally curdled in the making of tofu. You can also make your own soy buttermilk—just add two teaspoons of vinegar or lemon juice to one cup of soy milk.

Soy margarine: This is my everyday choice for table use. When I bake, I use oil in many of my recipes, but when only a good butter or margarine will do, I choose to use nondairy margarines and butters made from soybeans.

Grains

The new government food pyramid suggests that Americans eat plenty of whole grains as part of their overall diet. Whole grains may help reduce the risk of heart disease and certain cancers; they also provide the nutritional benefits of the entire grain: vitamins, minerals, dietary fiber, and other natural plant compounds called phytochemicals. When you're eating a whole-grain product, you're eating all the parts of the grain—the bran or outer layer, which is rich in fiber; the endosperm or middle part; and the germ or "wheat germ," the inner part, which is richest in nutrients. When grain is milled, or refined, as it is to produce many food products such as white bread, most pasta, and white flour, the bran and germ portions are removed, leaving only the endosperm. For optimum

health, you want to eat whole-grain foods that contain all three lay-
ers of the grain.

When you read a package label, you want to look for words
such as

- Whole wheat
- Whole barley
- Whole oats
- Cracked wheat
- Graham flour
- Whole cornmeal

What are your best bets in the grains category? For breakfast,
choose whole wheat cereals or oatmeal—a great way to boost your
daily fiber intake. Look for whole-grain products: cereal, brown rice,
wild rice, low-fat whole wheat crackers, popcorn, barley, and whole-
grain breads and rolls. I use brown basmati rice to make rice puddings, but you can use white basmati rice as well. The less
processed your rice is, the more nutrients it retains.

Flour

Many people bake only for special occasions or for the holidays, but
you may decide that regularly baking healthy treats for your kids
and *with* your kids is a terrific family activity you all can enjoy.
When it comes to baking, you've got lots of flour choices. Here's a
rundown of what's available and what I recommend.

Whole wheat flour contains wheat germ, which means that it
also has higher fiber, nutrition, and fat content. Because of the latter,
it should be stored in the refrigerator to prevent rancidity.

Whole-grain flour, like whole wheat pastry flour, is made from very soft wheat and milled into a fine flour. It's healthier than white flour but has less fiber than whole wheat flour. Do not substitute whole wheat flour for whole wheat pastry flour. The resulting cake will be more like dry bread.

Unbleached all-purpose white flour is a wheat flour that has been carefully milled into a white flour so it retains many of its original vitamins and minerals. It is not as refined as regular white flours, resulting in more fiber in the finished product.

Organic white flour is organically grown with no added chemicals.

Self-rising unbleached white flour is made from soft red wheat with salt and aluminum-free baking powder added. Do not add additional salt, baking powder, or baking soda when using self-rising flour. I do not suggest that you combine self-rising and unbleached white flours with other flours. Only use this in recipes that call for self-rising white flour.

Cake or pastry flour is a fine-textured, soft-wheat flour with a high starch content. It makes particularly tender cakes and pastries. Because it is more processed than other flours, I use it less frequently and only when it's called for in a special recipe.

Oat flour is made from groats that have been ground into powder. *It contains no gluten.* In baked goods that need to rise, like yeast bread, oat flour must be combined with a rising flour. Today, whole oats are still used as animal fodder. Human beings don't usually consume them until after the oats have been cleaned, toasted, hulled, and cleaned again, after which time they become oat groats.

Soy flour is made from roasted soybeans ground into a fine powder. There are three kinds of soy flour available: natural or full fat, which contains the natural oils found in the soybean; defatted, from which the oils are removed during processing; and lecithinated, which has added lecithin. This finely ground flour is made from soybeans and, unlike many flours, is high in protein (twice that of wheat flour) and low in carbohydrates. Soy flour is usually mixed with other flours rather than used alone. It has a wide variety of uses from baking desserts to binding sauces. In Japan, it's very popular for making confections. Soy flour is sold in health-food stores— sometimes under the name *kinako*—and in some supermarkets. I only use soy flour in recipes that are strong in flavor; I do not recommend using soy flour in plain cakes, pies, or muffins.

Fats

I used to hear the word *fat* and just cringe. When fat-free and low-fat desserts hit the market, I thought I was home free, as did a great many other Americans. I bought every fat-free product on the market, but none made me skinny. Disillusioned, I learned that most fat-free products reduced the fat but increased the sugar, sometimes as much as doubling or tripling it!

So what are "healthy" fats, and how should you be using them? I've discovered that different fats work best in different situations. I primarily use soy margarine and, on rare occasion, organic butter (see "Dairy"), and I cook with canola oil and some vegetable shortening. I always try to select the fat that will yield the best flavor and results while still allowing me to eat in a healthy way. I have worked hard to reduce the amount of fat in my recipes, and I've been pleased at how good they still taste.

The issue, though, is still reducing the amount of saturated fat in your diet. For this reason, manufacturers are making a real effort to eliminate trans-fatty acids from many packaged foods. What are they? Trans-fatty acids or trans fats are fats found in foods such as shortening and some margarines, as well as crackers, candies, baked goods, cookies, snack foods, fried foods, salad dressings, and many processed foods. Because scientists have proved there is a direct relationship between diets high in trans fat and rising LDL (bad) cholesterol levels, meaning an increased risk of coronary heart disease, the government is asking manufacturers to list the trans fat content in packaged foods.

How can you find out how much of this "unhealthy fat" is in a food you're considering at the store? Check the ingredient list on the food label. If you see the words *shortening, partially hydrogenated vegetable oil,* or *hydrogenated vegetable oil,* the food contains trans fat. Remember that ingredients are listed in descending order, so when the ingredient is close to the end of the list, it means the product contains a small amount.

Sugar

Not everyone agrees there is a clear connection between children's consumption of excessive amounts of sugar and hyperactive, distracted behavior. I've read a number of Internet articles and listened to reports on television that took the opposite position—that it's not the candy, cake, and ice cream served at birthday parties that seem to ignite off-the-wall behavior, but it's the nature of the events themselves. And a number of scientific studies have found it difficult to confirm *without doubt* that sugar is the culprit—*the only one*—in these situations.

My position is unchanged. I know from my research *and* from personal experience that refined sugar isn't nutritious, I also know that it supplies far too many calories in the diets of most children and adults, and I've collected pages of anecdotal evidence that my students are better behaved, more focused, and better able to understand what they're learning when they avoid high-sugar, high-fat foods. I'm convinced—as are their parents and teachers—that eliminating these unhealthy foods from school menus has been a good decision.

Remember, I've had the opportunity to observe hundreds of children on a daily basis, and while my personal research may not be as scientifically rigorous as a formal study, I'm satisfied that my community of students and their families have greatly benefited from our decision to create the Sugar-Free Zone at Browns Mill.

In the past several years, I've begun sharing my message with school districts and universities around the United States, and I can only report what they tell me: it's working for them, too. These results may not satisfy all the scientists, but there is no denying that the participants in these programs have experienced powerful transformations in body and mind.

Even experts agree that there's a lot we still don't know about how our bodies metabolize the food and drink we consume; part of that is because many children and adults don't respond exactly the same each time when they eat certain foods under scrutiny. Is this lack of certainty enough for them to conclude that sugar is not the reason for particular behaviors? For many, it is.

At the same time, the government is saying by way of its latest dietary guidelines that schools should be serving healthier foods and that families should be making healthier choices—eating less sugar, less salt, and less fat. Does it matter all that much whether sugar is worse for us than fat, or vice versa?

I don't think so.

There is plenty of proof that eating from the food pyramid and getting regular moderate exercise lowers your risk of developing diabetes, heart disease, and high blood pressure, three conditions whose numbers are dramatically rising in this country. So as the debate over sugar's role in disease and behavior continues, let's choose to eat well and get fit anyway!

SUGAR, SUGAR EVERYWHERE!

Did you know that in a recent year, each American consumed a record average of 154 pounds of sugar and other calorie sweeteners? It's true! That adds up to more than two-fifths of a pound of added sugar each and every day of the year. How much is that? Would you believe fifty-three teaspoons of added sugar per person, per day, all year long? You may be saying, someone's eating more than that because there's no way that I am, but you would be surprised to discover how much hidden sugar is in many common products, from bread to canned fruits to juice drinks marketed for children's consumption.

Now the government's recommended consumption of sugar is much lower—about six teaspoons per day for someone consuming about sixteen hundred calories daily, up to a maximum of about eighteen teaspoons of sugar. That is three times less than the study determined that people were actually eating!

If you're like most Americans, you're overeating sugar at a dangerous rate. A USDA report on food consumption suggests that as a nation we're consuming a toxic amount of sugar, and most of us don't even know it!

Where is all that sugar coming from? For many Americans, it's disguised in those big plastic bottles of favorite soft drinks and sodas. In 1986, for instance, people were drinking approximately twenty-eight gallons of soda per person per year; by 1997, it had escalated upward to forty-one gallons of soda. That breaks down to about 14.5 ounces of soda per person per day, which delivers the equivalent of eleven teaspoons of sugar all by itself!

Sweeteners: Artificial or Natural

When I was dieting, I used artificial sweeteners to reduce my sugar intake, and I purchased diet sodas and desserts. But these artificial sweeteners aren't necessarily healthy either, and in fact, recent studies suggest that they make it harder for us to distinguish when something is "sweet enough."

I don't use white sugar or similar refined sweeteners in any of my recipes because I believe that white sugars have no nutritive value. To make these products, the juice extracted from the sugar cane goes through a bleaching process that helps to whiten the sugar. During the refining process, which produces the fine granular product we find on store shelves, white sugar loses most of its nutrients, which means that the calories it provides deliver very little nourishment.

One way it has changed me is that I have stopped eating candy. Now I feel healthier. I can do more things now. A sugar-free school should occur in all schools.

In the past I used to eat a lot of candy; now I have stopped that. I have shown my whole family what it means to be sugar-free. Since I'm healthy, I have more energy now. This school has made me feel more at home. Now I eat the right servings every day. All of my cousins eat candy, but if they had a sugar-free school, things would change. It has also changed my life by making me have a better mind. I hope it can change other people's lives, too.

—Antonio, third grade

Natural Sweeteners

Natural sweeteners are alternatives to white and refined sugars. When natural sweeteners are used, you can usually reduce the amount of sugar in a recipe by a third, and sometimes even by half. Unlike white sugar, natural sweeteners have no additives or preservatives. I experimented with many different natural sweeteners before I decided which ones worked best for me. Most of my recipes require dry (granulated) sweeteners such as maple sugar, turbinado sugar, or organic sugar. Liquid sweeteners such as maple syrup, unsulphured molasses, and natural, sugar-free fruit juices also work well in some recipes. I would not suggest the use of liquid sweeteners as a substitute for dry sweeteners unless specified in the recipe. Also remember that some liquid natural sweeteners, while healthy, can be high in calories. For instance, I choose not to use honey because it is sweeter than white sugar and works just like white sugar does in my body: it makes me crave other sugars and carbohydrates.

Remember also that all sugars are *not* natural sugars. Brown sugar, for example, is not a natural sugar. It is the same as white sugar, except it has had molasses added for color, flavor, and texture.

Confused about sweeteners? Here's a quick rundown of best bets:

Maple sugar, which is twice as sweet as granulated white sugar, is the result of continuing to boil maple tree sap until the liquid has almost entirely evaporated. Turbinado sugar, which can be found under the brand name of Sugar in the Raw, is sugar that has been steam cleaned. The coarse turbinado crystals are blond colored and have a delicate molasses flavor. Why is this a healthier choice? It's just not as processed as refined white sugar. It's also absorbed into the bloodstream more slowly, so it doesn't cause your blood sugar to rise as rapidly as white sugar. In my recipes, this is what I mean by natural sugar. Fruits as sweeteners are a very healthy option, so I use natural and frozen fruits in many of my recipes. I only use frozen fruits that do not contain preservatives or added sugars.

Florida Crystal is a very fine natural cane sugar that is harvested and milled the same day. Use it as you would superfine sugar—in delicate cakes and cheesecakes.

Try different products with your family and decide which ones you like best. Never allow your concerns about health let you forget that "life is sweet"!

If You Need Reasons to Give Up Sugar . . .

A few years ago, I found a list on the Web, created by Dr. Nancy Appleton, called "78 Ways Sugar Can Ruin Your Health." Well, when I went looking for the site again so I could include the URL in this book, I saw the list had grown to 124, which didn't surprise me one bit. For the entire list, go to www.NancyAppleton.com, but here are just a few *really* good reasons to eliminate sugar from your diet:

1. Sugar can suppress the immune system.

4. Sugar can produce a significant rise in triglycerides.

13. Sugar can weaken eyesight.

19. Sugar can cause premature aging.

66. Sugar can increase the body's fluid retention.

71. Sugar can cause headaches, including migraine.

107. Sugar can worsen the symptoms of children with attention deficit hyperactivity disorder (ADHD).

Other Cooking and Baking Ingredients

Here are some other common ingredients likely to be used in dishes you prepare for your family. This list is by no means complete, but it's worth your time to learn about the ingredients that will help you produce healthier homemade food.

Applesauce (unsweetened): Unsweetened applesauce can be used to reduce oil in many recipes. It's particularly good in muffins and quick breads.

Baking powder: I suggest using only aluminum-free baking powder.

Chocolates and carob: Some say the creation of chocolate was the beginning of sin, but I believe that it was the making of heaven! I do use chocolate in some of my recipes, but when I do, I use unsweetened chocolate, natural semisweetened chocolate, or unsweetened Dutch-processed cocoa. People who refrain from eating chocolate use carob as a substitute. The long, leathery pods from the tropical carob tree contain a sweet, edible pulp that can be eaten fresh and a few hard, inedible seeds. After drying, the pulp is roasted and ground into a powder. It is then used to flavor baked goods and candies. Both fresh and dried carob pods, as well as carob powder, may be found in health-food and specialty-food stores. Because carob is sweet and tastes something like chocolate, it's commonly used as a chocolate substitute.

Coconut: I recommend using unsweetened coconut flakes, dried unsweetened coconut, or frozen unsweetened coconut. But coconut is high in fat and should be used in moderation.

Extracts: I use natural and regular extracts instead of imitation flavors in all of my recipes. You can also use nonalcoholic extracts.

Gelatins: When I am making dairy-free recipes that require gelatin, I will use kosher gelatin. I also use an unsweetened, store-brand, unflavored gelatin in some recipes.

Peanut butter: I only use natural peanut butter, with no added sugar. If oil has accumulated on the top, stir before using.

Salt: I do not use regular salt, only iodized sea salt, when I cook. I also recommend other salt-free condiments like Mrs. Dash.

Now, What about Water?

Most people don't consume nearly enough. Here are some facts about our need for water that may help you and your children break your soda habit!

Did you know:

- You cannot survive without water.
- Water can provide essential nutrients and minerals you need for health.

THE "SUPERFOODS" THAT BOOST YOUR BRAIN AND BODY

Recent research has trumpeted a list of what scientists are calling "mind-nourishing foods," foods that actually help the brain function better when it's engaged in learning. As an educator, I'd be a fool not to take this list and run with it, and I'm no fool! We use most of these ingredients in our school menus (reserving the tea for adults only), and the results speak for themselves: healthier, higher achieving students who have an advantage over other kids because they have learned to feed their minds while feeding their bodies!

Beans	Soy
Blueberries	Spinach
Broccoli	Tea (green or black)
Oats	Tomatoes
Oranges	Turkey
Pumpkin	Walnuts
Salmon	Yogurt

- Water makes up two-thirds of your total body weight. Our most precious organs and tissues are mainly water:
  - brain—70 percent water
  - muscles—73 percent water
  - blood—82 percent water
  - lungs—90 percent water
- Eight glasses of water each day really will help keep the doctor away.
- Water has no calories.
- Water increases mental clarity and concentration in children and adults.
- Water helps to hydrate the brain and deepen comprehension.
- Water suppresses the appetite.
- Water helps rid the body of unwanted fat and toxins.
- Water is a great defense against gaining unwanted pounds.

Nothing else you consume does you as much good as water does! So drink up!

I like to be sugar-free because it helps me stay healthy. I eat fruit so I can have lots of energy. I eat a healthy breakfast, lunch, and dinner. You can focus on your work at school and move on to the next grade. It's great to be sugar-free. You can get rotten teeth if you eat too much candy. You can get cavities by eating candy. There are lots of ways to be sugar-free.

I love being sugar-free! It's my thing! Sugar-free rocks! I think you would want to be sugar-free too. Go sugar-free! I want to be sugar-free for the rest of my life!

—*Aliyah, second grade*

WHAT ELSE DO CHILDREN NEED TO SUCCEED? ZZZZZZZZZZZZ

Besides a healthy diet, children need SLEEP—at least eight or nine hours a night is best so they can perform well in school. If your children need to be up at 6:30 or 7 AM for school, this means that they should be in bed before 10 PM. Younger children may need even more rest after a busy day. Children who are well rested are more alert than overtired kids who must depend on sugar and adrenaline to get them through the school day.

Food Allergies

It's a sobering fact that more than 11 million Americans suffer from food allergies, and physicians report that this figure is on the rise. Are we becoming more sensitive to what's in what we eat, or are we simply getting better at diagnosing our myriad sensitivities to a wide range of popular foods?

It's a good question, and as yet not fully answered. In the meantime, concern about food allergies has influenced school and restaurant menus and even what's served on commercial jets. Recipe ingredients and prepared food products are now more carefully scrutinized, so no one unwittingly consumes a product that may cause a life-threatening allergic reaction. Many airlines have replaced the traditional packets of peanuts, for example, with pretzels or cheese crackers because those with nut allergies can become ill even if they inhale a bit of "nut dust" in the airplane cabin. Menus carry detailed ingredient lists to help consumers make safer choices; it's not uncommon for chefs to include unusual items in their special dishes, from peanut butter in chili to fish oils in sauces.

The most common food allergens are peanuts, tree nuts (walnuts, pecans, etc.), fish, shellfish, eggs, milk, soy, and wheat. Peanuts are the leading cause of severe allergic reactions, followed by all kinds of shellfish and fish, tree nuts, and eggs.

If you have an allergy, or if a member of your family has one, you already know about the effort it takes to read labels on packaged foods and ask all those questions of your server before ordering restaurant meals. For those who cope daily with these allergies, there is often a deep sense of deprivation as they watch others eat whatever they want. This kind of deprivation can be especially hard on children, who often have to eat special meals at school or must bring their own treats to birthday parties and other gatherings.

As a parent, I've had plenty of firsthand experience with a child's food allergies. My husband and I are the proud parents of a wonderful son, Denard, whose difficulties inspired many of the recipes in my cookbook, *Dessert Lovers' Choice: Naturally Sweet, Naturally Delicious.* From the day he was born, he cried constantly, and we couldn't imagine why this beautiful baby was so miserable.

When Denard was four weeks old, we found out that he was allergic to milk. With the help of our pediatrician, we tried a number of formulas, but none of them worked for our son. Finally, the doctor recommended that we try giving him soy milk, an uncommon prescription for that time. I prayed that this formula would be just what he needed, and my prayers were answered—Denard responded well to the soy milk, and we thought that our problems were over.

But the next few years were very hard on our family. Whenever my son visited his grandmother's farm, he experienced allergic reactions to fresh hen eggs, and we soon discovered that he was also allergic to anything that contained corn. Besides his food allergies, he also was diagnosed with asthma.

As he grew, I had to learn fast about the ways that food affected him. I packed his lunch every morning, careful to give him minimally processed foods—natural applesauce, boxes of raisins, and turkey sandwiches on whole wheat bread. Even those healthy foods caused Denard problems. I found out that he was also allergic to wheat and reacted badly to dairy products and anything containing red dye.

Like many children with serious allergies, Denard accepted the limits on what he could eat, but as more and more foods were denied him, he felt the urge to rebel against the constraints of his bland diet. It's not hard to understand. He couldn't even have popcorn when he went to the movies! Occasionally during school lunch he would deliberately grab a container of chocolate milk, but his classmates alerted his teacher, who had asked the other students to help keep an eye on students with dietary concerns.

I'd believed and hoped that by removing all his problem foods from his diet, Denard would outgrow his allergies, as some children do. But he was not so lucky. How could I, as his mother, make it better for him? I didn't want him to miss out on all those sweet treats of childhood, so I started developing healthy recipes for goodies he could eat without fear of becoming ill.

I started by replacing regular milk in recipes with soy milk, to which he'd always responded well. I was very familiar with the product, since I was lactose intolerant myself. Now there are so many great products that offer soy alternatives to regular dairy items that we never have to feel deprived, and soy ice cream, for instance, comes in lots of great flavors.

To help my son resist the temptation of what I called "no-no" desserts, I created recipes for cakes, cookies, smoothies, and even homemade ice cream treats. I also developed my own healthy snacks that appealed to all kids, not just those who weren't allowed to eat the usual stuff. You'll find a terrific selection of our favorites in the recipe section in chapter 6.

If you're a parent whose children suffer from food allergies or experience a lesser form, such as food intolerance or hypersensitivity, you've got even more reason to study food labels obsessively. Did you know that some children's vitamins contain lactose? Or that some products that contain hydrogenated vegetable oil or hydrolyzed vegetable protein may be made with casein, which is a milk derivative? If your child has problems with dairy, you should also know that many over-the-counter medications contain lactose as a binder, as do some brands of tuna fish.

Here are several useful Web sites for parents whose children have food allergies. You'll also find that many parents have created their own Web sites on the subject, with information on products that have caused problems for their own children—and products that their kids love.

The Food Allergy Network
www.foodallergy.org/index.html

The No Milk Page
www.panix.com/ ~ nomilk/

Lactose Intolerance Clearinghouse
http://ourworld.compuserve.com/homepages/stevecarper

Keep Kids Healthy Network (a pediatrician's guide to
your children's health and safety)
**www.keepkidshealthy.com/welcome/commonproblems/food_
allergies.html**

At www.askdrsears.com, pediatrician and best-selling author
Dr. Bill Sears offers detailed information for parents on the subject of
food allergies in children, including how to recognize that your child
may be having problems with certain foods. He points out that parents who have food allergies or sensitivities are very likely to have
children who experience allergic reactions, though not necessarily to
the same foods. Is there anything you can do?

Current research suggests that if mothers don't consume problem
foods during their pregnancy, it can help their children later on. Breast-
feeding is also supposed to help keep your child from developing food
allergies; it coats the intestinal lining with a substance called im-
munoglobulin that keeps allergens from getting into the bloodstream.

Many physicians also recommend that you delay introducing
solid foods, especially those containing soy, dairy, and wheat, before
the body is prepared to handle them; the baby may become allergic
to those foods later on. That's one of the reasons babies are started
on fruits and vegetables that cause the fewest allergies later on. In-
terestingly, Dr. Sears notes that citrus fruits shouldn't be introduced
until much later on. Sears also shares my belief that it's best to avoid
giving your child foods with dyes and colorings.

How can you tell if your child may have a food allergy? Watch for symptoms such as hives; red, sandpaper-like facial rash; dry, scaly, itchy skin (mostly on face); swelling in hands and feet; puffy eyelids; dark circles under eyes; tongue soreness; wheezing; watery eyes; persistent cough; congestion; recurring ear infections; abdominal discomfort; diarrhea; constipation; intestinal bleeding; bloating; gassiness; vomiting; migraine headaches; hyperactivity; night waking; anxiety; crankiness; and sore muscles and joints.

Here are two lists of foods—the first, containing foods most likely to produce allergic reactions, and the second, containing those you and your children can consume with little concern about a possible reaction.

More Allergenic

- berries
- buckwheat
- chocolate
- cinnamon
- citrus fruits
- coconut
- corn
- dairy products
- egg whites
- mustard
- nuts
- peanut butter
- peas
- pork
- shellfish
- soy
- sugar
- tomatoes
- wheat
- yeast

Least Allergenic

- apples
- apricots
- asparagus
- avocados
- barley
- beets
- broccoli
- carrots

- cauliflower
- chicken
- cranberries
- dates
- grapes
- lamb
- lettuce
- mangoes
- oats
- papayas
- peaches
- pears

- poi
- raisins
- rice
- rye
- safflower oil
- salmon
- squash
- sunflower oil
- sweet potatoes
- turkey
- veal

Note: When you read food labels, watch for these terms that may "disguise" problem foods:

- wheat flour: durum, semolina, farina
- egg: albumin
- dairy products: casein, sodium caseinate.

As a student with diabetes, the Sugar-Free Zone has helped me to organize how I eat at school and at home. The cafeteria staff helps me to stay healthy and my parents appreciate that.

The importance of staying healthy as a diabetic means you have to make sure your diet is balanced. I thank this school and everyone for supporting this healthy program and me.

—Lydia, sixth grade

Setting the Stage for Success 5

Preparing Your Home, Shopping,
Recommended Products,
Reading Food Labels, and Putting
It All into Action

Now that I've shared with you about what
we've been doing at Browns Mill and why it's working, plus some
helpful information that we've learned along the way, it's time for
you to begin making changes in your home, and probably in your at-
titudes about food as well. It's very difficult to change what you've
been doing for a long time because you're on a kind of automatic
pilot. You may be used to shopping in a sort of daze, picking up
familiar packages without paying much attention to healthier alternatives. Perhaps you've been struggling for years with your own
weight and unconsciously passing along some of your negative
habits to your children. Or maybe you are like so many other Americans, stuck on a kind of treadmill that's hard to get off—eating fast
food, skipping meals, not moving nearly enough.

Well, STOP.

Say the word out loud and see if it sounds like a wake-up call.
The first step in making positive changes is to stop what you're doing wrong. Once you've done that, you're ready to fix what isn't
working. But that requires awareness, a willingness to pay close at-

tention to what you do and what you think when it comes to food. I know you can do it. I don't want you to wait for the kind of wake-up call I got, and if you and your family can follow the advice in this book, you won't have to!

Now that I have your attention, it's time to start fresh. One of the best ways to do that is to prepare your house for living under a new administration. You'll want to clean out your cabinets of outdated and unhealthy products, you'll need to stock your pantry and refrigerator with a selection of better choices, and you'll want to increase your understanding of healthier behaviors by learning more about what your family needs for optimum health.

Let's begin.

Get Rid of It! Purging Your Kitchen of Foods That Just Aren't Healthy

Now that you've made the commitment to giving your family foods that deliver the best possible nutrition, it's time to eliminate from your shelves common food products that stand in your way. The products listed below are full of empty calories and unhealthy ingredients. In many cases, what may have begun as nutritious foods lose their nutrients in the manufacturing process.

Take bread, for instance: if the whole grain kernel has been removed, so has most of the nutrition. While many refined grain products have been fortified with iron and the B vitamins, like thiamine, niacin, riboflavin, and folic acid, the fiber is usually not replaced. Fiber plays a powerful role in preventing disease and promoting better health, so choosing foods that are high in fiber just makes better sense.

Make this cleanup a family affair; it's a great way to educate your kids about what's in the foods they eat and what foods are best avoided when your goals are good health and high energy.

Get Rid of	Use Instead
White flour White rice White bread	Whole grains: whole wheat flour, whole cornmeal, couscous, barley, bulgur wheat, rye, oatmeal, brown rice, whole wheat bread, rye bread
White sugar	Fruit juices, raisins, applesauce, or raw (turbinado) sugar to sweeten foods
Hard margarine (which contains hydrogenated fatty acids that can raise cholesterol)	Soybean and safflower oil margarines that are free of trans fats
High-fat, high-refined sugar cookies and chips	Homemade versions using whole-grain flours or healthier versions (Read the food labels!)
High-fat, high-sugar ice cream	Frozen juice bars and nondairy confections, or make your own
Sweetened carbonated sodas, sugary fruit drinks and soft drinks (which dehydrate children and may contribute to weight gain and hypertension)	Bottled or purified water, homemade lemonade or limeade from fresh fruit

Stocking Your Pantry

Here's a quick and handy list of items that are good to have on hand—in your cabinets, in the freezer, on a pantry shelf. Don't over-buy, of course. Too much of a good thing can make you feel over-crowded and overwhelmed. Please note: this list consists of foods that you can store and keep on hand, not the fresh produce and meats you need to shop for more often. In this section, I suggest foods in every category that have a longer shelf, refrigerator, or freezer life.

Breads and Grains

- Whole-grain bread (three grams of fiber per serving)
- Pasta (whole wheat, rice)
- Rice (basmati, Arborio, jasmine, and brown rice)
- Fortified whole-grain cereal (at least three grams of fiber per serving)
- Fresh or frozen whole-grain pizza crust
- Frozen whole-grain waffles or pancakes
- Tortillas
- Sandwich wraps (Different flavors are fun!)
- Pretzels (unsalted or low salt; skinny are better than thick and doughy)
- Other grains: kashi, quinoa, couscous, wheat germ (instead of bread crumbs)

Vegetables

Root Vegetables

These should be stored in a cool, dry place and will keep longer than other vegetables. However, the sooner you use them, the more nutrients they will deliver.

- Potatoes (baking, sweet, new, red, even gourmet potatoes like fingerling or purple Peruvian for a new taste sensation!)
- Onions (Spanish, Vidalia, Maui)
- Carrots
- Turnips, rutabagas, parsnips (whatever local farmers offer at the market)

Frozen Vegetables

Because they are usually "flash frozen" right after being picked, frozen vegetables can be a healthy option. In fact, they may deliver more nutrition than fresh vegetables that have traveled a long way or that have been sitting in grocery store bins for many days after being picked. Prepare these with as little water as possible to retain nutrients.

Some good choices include:

- Peas
- Corn
- Chopped broccoli
- Italian green beans
- String beans
- Carrots
- Bags of international blends

Fruit

Your best bet is to choose fresh fruit whenever possible, but it's also smart to have selected canned and frozen fruit products on hand. Choose canned fruit in its own juice, or if you can only find a product in light or heavy syrup, rinse it and drain before eating. (Mandarin oranges usually require this.) Frozen fruits—especially berries, melon pieces, and peaches—are great to keep on hand for use in smoothies. Choose only fruit that has *no sugar added*. Thawed, it can be substituted for fresh in many recipes. Just be sure to drain it well.

Proteins

You've read earlier about fresh proteins—meat, fish, poultry, and tofu. You will need to shop for those more frequently, but you can

---

TEST-TAKING SUCCESS SECRETS—THE WORD IS OUT!

Healthy eating is an important key to higher test scores for our Browns Mill students. But then we up the ante when it really counts. We have a special menu on every testing day. What do the kids demand because they know it works? Red grapes, sugarless mints, and lemon drops!

Researchers have found that red grapes are brain food—able to help protect the brain from strokes because they contain resveratrol, an antioxidant that's shown a remarkable list of health benefits. It keeps blood from clotting and plugging up arteries, it lowers blood pressure, and it appears to help prevent cancer. Of particular interest to our students? It's been shown to promote the formation of new connections between brain cells, and the more connections, the more memory remains intact as you age.

So don't let the kids have all the benefits of this amazing fruit—share it with your family!

The mints and lemon drops? Well, peppermint is highly recommended for the digestive, nervous, respiratory, and immune systems. And lemon also helps to settle the digestive system. Instead of suffering on test day with their stomachs in knots, our students are cool, calm, and collected—and SMART!

---

also buy fresh and then freeze protein until you're ready to use it. Just remember, the longer it sits in your freezer, the more likely an item in this category will lose texture, taste, and, yes, even some nutrients. As a good backup, try keeping some of these canned and frozen protein foods on hand.

Canned
- Tuna fish in water
- Salmon
- Crabmeat
- Chunk chicken
- Beans (kidney, pinto, cannellini, great northern, navy, garbanzo)

Frozen

If you buy any of these fresh, I recommend that before freezing, divide large packages into individual portions so that you only have to defrost as much as you need for a meal.

- Boneless, skinless chicken breasts
- Frozen precooked shrimp
- Fish fillets
- Whole turkey breast
- Ground turkey breast, ground chicken, ground lean beef
- Veggie burgers

Canned Tomatoes and Soups

You'll notice that I don't recommend stocking canned vegetables in your healthy pantry. Why? Many canned foods contain excess amounts of sodium, so if you choose to purchase veggies processed in this manner, choose brands that contain less than five hundred milligrams of sodium per serving. If you can't find what you need in a low-sodium version, then rinse the vegetables well. One vegetable that you do need and want to stock in canned form is tomatoes. (See below for the news about lycopene!) I always have plenty on hand in these three forms:

- Crushed tomatoes
- Tomato purée
- Whole tomatoes

I also recommend stocking up on these soup products, many of which you'll find in delicious versions at your best source for healthy products.

- Low fat soups (vegetable based, fat-free, low fat)
- Low-fat, low-sodium chicken, beef, or vegetable stock

• • • • • • • • • • • • • • • • • • • •

Research suggests that phytochemicals known as carotenoids are better absorbed from cooked rather than raw foods. These powerful antioxidants are present in red, orange, and yellow vegetables and fruits. Lycopene, a phytochemical shown to fight cancer, is more available in cooked tomato products, such as canned or stewed tomatoes, pasta sauces, and ketchup. Carrots also have higher levels of beta-carotene after cooking. And corn's antioxidant activity increases the longer you cook it!

• • • • • • • • • • • • • • • • • • • •

Fats

These are the fats I always have on hand. Carefully stored, they will keep for quite a long time.

- Extra virgin olive oil
- Canola oil
- Nonstick cooking spray

Condiments

- Low-sodium bouillon cubes or packets
- Low-sodium soy sauce
- Mayonnaise (fat-free or reduced fat)
- Salad dressing (fat-free or reduced fat)
- Lemon and/or lime juice
- Salsa and picante sauce
- Relish
- Mustard
- Ketchup
- Balsamic vinegar, rice vinegar, red wine vinegar
- Low-sugar jelly, jam, or spreadable fruit

- Natural extracts (lemon, vanilla, almond, coconut, mint)
- Mrs. Dash
- Chili powder, garlic powder

Beverages

Don't wait to drink until you are thirsty. Also remember that once you've met your daily requirement for calcium, your best choice of beverage is still water.

Freezer

- 100 percent juices
- Sugar-free lemonade

Pantry

- Canned juices (choose low-sodium versions of tomato juice, and look for no-sugar-added versions of any fruit juices)

Refrigerator

- Milk (low-fat or fat-free), soy milk, rice milk
- Sparkling water, fruit-flavored water, vitamin water
- 100 percent juices
- Iced tea (sugar-free), fruit teas

Healthy Substitutions

A key to eating healthy for a lifetime is finding delicious substitutes for foods your family enjoys but that are not high in fat and/or sugar. Here's a quick list of ways to please the palate without giving up favorite flavors:

Instead of Eating	Try This
Sausage, bacon	Lean ham, turkey, or sausage, or Canadian bacon
Ground beef	Ground turkey breast, ground chicken breast
Tuna in oil	Tuna in water
Whole eggs	Egg whites, egg substitute
Cream cheese	Low-fat cottage cheese, yogurt
Cream (in recipes)	Nonfat yogurt
Sugary cereals, granola	Unsweetened cereals topped with fresh fruit or fruit sauces
Potato chips, corn chips	Pretzels, low-fat crackers
Donuts, pastries at breakfast	Whole-grain toast with low-sugar jam and/or low-fat cream cheese
Ice cream	Sorbet, low-fat ice cream, soy ice cream
Cream soups	Nonfat chicken broth

Shopping

Soon we may all be able to order our groceries over the Internet, but just in case you still need to pile the kids into the car and head for the nearest supermarket, here are my tips for making this weekly chore a positive—and educational—experience for the entire family.

If you can take the time, even if it's not *every* time, food shopping trips can be a wonderful chance for discovery and learning for your young children. You'll find that there are opportunities for your

NOTHING LASTS FOREVER

American manufacturers keep improving the packaging of grocery items, but that doesn't mean you can keep food forever. Just because something looks fresh in your refrigerator doesn't mean it's still good—or good for you. Always check the "use by" date that appears on most products, but here's *my* rule: *If you can't remember when you bought it, it's probably time to get rid of it!*

These guidelines will help you keep your food fresh and your family healthy:

Refrigerator Item	Keep It for
Juices in cartons (open)	7–10 days
Hard cheese (cheddar, Swiss)	3–4 weeks
Milk	7 days
Yogurt	7–14 days
Raw egg yolks and whites	2–4 days
Liquid pasteurized eggs or egg substitute	3 days
Half-and-half	3–4 days
Ground beef or turkey	1–2 days
Hot dogs	1 week
Lunch meats	3–5 days
Nondairy whipped cream (aerosol can)	3 months
Real whipped cream (aerosol can)	3–4 weeks
Store-prepared egg, meat, or pasta salads	3–5 days
Mayonnaise	2 months

children to learn new vocabulary (literacy) as they walk through the aisles with you, calculate percentages of nutrients (math), understand where in the world different foods are imported from (geography, social studies), and even discuss how fresh foods such as milk or produce can spoil (science, health). You're sure to find all kinds of "teachable moments" during your visits to the store, but here are a few ideas to get you and your family started:

• Write out your shopping list together. This not only reinforces what your child may be learning in school about nutrition and different kinds of foods but will also teach your child something about menu planning, the major food groups, and the concept that different ingredients go into the preparation of a single dish or meal.

• Let your child choose one or two new foods for the family to try. Encourage your child to focus on fresh fruits and vegetables as well as different kinds of low-fat snacks. Children who help select grocery items are likely to remain interested in their selections. If your daughter chooses a new kind of melon or type of apple, she will probably look forward to trying it and ask for it when snack or dessert time arrives.

• Make each shopping trip a discovery experience; treat it like an expedition of sorts into unknown territory, and even consider helping your child draw a map of the store, including what's in what aisle, and so on. Encourage your child to experience the variety of foods that are grown or produced in this country or around the world.

• Make time, if you can, to talk about and experience numbers—ounces in a box of cereal, volume of milk in a container, or cost per pound of different items. Have your child use the produce scale to weigh your selections; point out shelf labels that give information about cost per ounce, so he/she can practice comparing items to find the best value. Your child can also practice estimating how many bags of groceries you'll load into the trunk, and shopping offers good opportunities for children to learn about equivalents— how two pints equal a quart, and why two small cans may contain less and cost more than one larger can.

• Before you go and during your visit, study food labels together (see the next section for more on this). It's a great way to carry on a continual dialogue about what's *in* what we eat, and why it matters so much!

• After your shopping trip, unpack the groceries together. Younger children can sort items by where they will be stored, while older children can work on recognizing letters and words on familiar and unfamiliar packages. Talk about the components of a healthy meal and which foods the family should eat daily.

Shopping Smart in Those "Miles of Aisles"

Many people may not realize that supermarkets are designed to make us buy, buy, buy—capitalizing on the fact that we're usually hungry, tired, saddled with distracted children, or thinking about anything else but food when we shop. But it's no longer a secret: supermarkets are scientifically designed to get you to spend more! From the music to the aromas, they're aiming to tempt you into trying new products, buying more than you need (in giant-size packages), and generally manipulating you to do what *they* want, not what you want.

To keep your spending down and avoid those impulse items that are not part of your healthy eating program, you need a PLAN!

• Don't shop on an empty stomach. Hunger pangs can have a bad influence on what you are buying.

• Shop with a list, preferably arranged by aisle or area of the store, so you can cover the territory you need to without spending the night.

• Concentrate on the outside edges of the supermarket where the healthiest foods tend to be located—the milk and juices, the produce, the meats, and, depending on the store, the frozen-food section. You have to dive into the middle aisles in most cases to find the chips, cookies, and sugary cereals.

• Know which middle aisles you need to hit to pick up canned beans and vegetables, healthy broths and soups, brown rice, whole wheat pastas and cereals, canned fruit, and jarred condiments.

• When buying bread, don't be easily seduced by signs that trumpet "whole grain." Check to be sure each one-slice serving contains at least three grams of fiber.

• The last stop should be the frozen section so that whatever you buy doesn't thaw before you get it home. Best bets here are frozen vegetables, which are usually flash frozen right after they are harvested and tend to retain their nutrients better than some fresh products that have traveled far and long to get to your produce department. Avoid products that are cooked in sauces; these tend to be high in fat and/or sugar.

• One last tip: wear comfortable shoes when you shop. If your feet hurt, you'll be more susceptible to rushing through without taking the time to choose the healthiest options.

Shopping by Season

Even as adults, we find ourselves influenced by the traditional unfolding of the school year. We never quite lose the memory, bred in the bone, of how it feels to prepare for the start of school. September arrives, and we feel the urge to buy new notebooks and sharpen pencils. December arrives with the promise of a holiday vacation. March heralds the arrival of spring and the chance to spend more time outside, while June makes us restless for the long nights of summer and time for fun.

Once we "tune ourselves in" to the rhythms of the growing seasons, we discover that they, too, inspire us to crave different foods at different times of the year. By eating naturally, choosing fresh foods when they are at their ripest, we find a kind of pleasure in healthy eating we may never have realized before.

I've already established how important fruits and vegetables are as components of a good nutrition plan for you and your family. These foods are high in fiber and rich in taste satisfaction—crunch, texture, even aroma. They can also help to curb overeating, in part because they take time to consume properly and allow for the body to experience the sensations of fullness and satisfaction.

Fruits and vegetables are nutrient dense, packed with vitamins and minerals we need to operate on all cylinders! And we get the best values from them by "eating in the moment," selecting from the freshest gifts of each season as the year rolls by. As federal dietary guidelines increase the number of servings per day recommended for a healthy diet, it's becoming more important to bring the bounty of each season to your table.

Fall: Rich in yellows and oranges, the produce of autumn echoes the changing colors of the trees outside your windows. Fall offers a splendid harvest of vegetables to select from, especially Brussels sprouts, cabbage, sweet potatoes, pumpkin, cucumbers, onions, and squash such as zucchini and yellow squash. It's also the season for crisp, red apples; cantaloupes and other melons; red and purple grapes; pears of every shade, from golden yellow to deep russet; and some varieties of oranges. These nutritional "bargains" are great sources of vitamin A, vitamin C, and potassium. A perfect fall family excursion is a trip to the nearest orchards. Pick as many apples as you can carry, and make homemade applesauce together on a chilly weekend afternoon!

Winter: As hardy as the season itself, winter vegetables sustain us through the coldest, darkest months of the year. This season's essentials include rosy beets, carrots, spinach, winter squash, various greens, broccoli and cauliflower, and all kinds of dried beans, peas, and other legumes. Winter is a great time for citrus fruits such as grapefruit and oranges, but it's also a wonderful time to enjoy baked fruits—particularly apples and pears, which have so much natural sweetness all they require is a sprinkle of cinnamon and some time in the oven or microwave. A little sugar-free syrup is also good! These cozy winter fruits and vegetables provide us with the B complex vitamins so vital to healthy living.

Spring: Oh, how we welcome this season of renewal, when the coats come off, the windows go up, and the children can play outside for hours! It's always energizing to spot the first appearance of those vegetables we associate with spring. Asparagus, lush lettuces of every variety, and pale green celery are just a few. And once those rubies called strawberries begin to appear in May, it's not unusual to feel like buying half a dozen pints to use in smoothies, on top of cereal, or just eat by the handful. Watch for Valencia oranges and luscious lemons, perfect for squeezing into fresh lemonade and orangeade. Even your children will notice the difference in flavor.

Summer: As the temperature rises, so do the number and variety of fresh produce available to us at farmers' markets and in our grocery stores. Irresistible summer veggies include green beans; corn; ripe red tomatoes from plum to heirloom, cherry to beefsteak; and the special gift of the season, sweet corn. Now is the time to eat peaches, plums, watermelon, and, for a brief time in August, dark sweet cherries. Eat these spectacular summer varieties at their ripest to enjoy their nutritional benefits. The more we consume of these, the better to keep our hearts healthy, our blood pressure and cholesterol low, and our weight in check.

Being in a sugar-free school has helped me a lot! I make sure that the food or drink that I'm eating or drinking says "100 percent." I walk a lot now! I don't like a lot of candy and other sweets anymore. I think it's a good idea to have a sugar-free school. I would like to thank Dr. Butler for making this a sugar-free school! Some people don't like being sugar-free. Some people don't like being healthy. The same people may one day get diabetes. Now that I am sugar-free, I can fight the chances of being obese and getting diabetes!

—*Symon, third grade*

Some Recommended Products

As consumers everywhere continue to request healthier products in every food category, you're sure to see even more choices in your supermarkets and grocery stores. Until then, you may have to patronize local health food stores to find the products you prefer.

But here's what I told the parents of my students: If you don't see what you want, *ask for it*. When there is a demand for a new product, it makes good business sense for the store to stock it, whether you shop at Piggly Wiggly or Vons, at Costco or Wal-mart. Many stores in the smallest towns in America now carry organic vegetables, fresh and frozen; a larger assortment of low-sugar as well as low-fat products; and a growing number of healthy snacks from large and small manufacturers. Soon there will be even more than there are now! (And isn't that good news!)

Here are some of my suggestions for foods and snacks that will help your family enjoy a healthier lifestyle every day! But you'll want to check these out—read the food labels—for yourself.

LOST IN A HEALTH-FOOD STORE?

Have you had the experience of wandering into a health food store and feeling utterly confused by the merchandise? Oh, some items are recognizable, but you've probably found yourself asking, "What is spelt bread?" or "Is brown rice pasta better for you than the regular kind?"

Have you wondered what was in all those serve-yourself bins of mysterious-looking nuts, beans, seeds, and powdery flours? Have you gazed at shelves of cereals, studied racks of snacks, and even peered into the freezer case, uncertain whether to pick up a pint of Rice Dream ice cream or a vegetarian entrée? Confused, frustrated, or just overwhelmed by the choices, you may have walked right out without buying a thing!

The good news is that health-food stores are becoming more user-friendly, especially as the lines between their products and what is available at your supermarket have become more and more blurred. Even drugstores have begun carrying lines of natural food products, making it not only easier to find them locally but also to save money by finding the best prices on products you and your family enjoy.

In the following section, I've listed some of my favorite natural products—family approved, kid tested, and easy to incorporate into your menus at home. This section is by no means complete, especially as new products enter the marketplace every week, or at least that's the way it seems! Don't feel that you have to replace everything in your cupboard when you decide to start making healthier choices for yourself and your kids. Start with a few new products at a time—substitute a box of Oatios for your traditional dry cereal, sample new snacks such as Veggie Booty or Barbara's Bakery Cheese Puffs while watching a football game together, and as your confidence builds, pick an aisle or two to explore each month or so. You'll find lots of healthy versions of products you already use, and you'll also learn about options for adding uncommon but delicious grain products to your menu, foods such as quinoa or amaranth. You'll also discover the many options you have in using vegetable-based protein products—from the widely distributed Boca Burger brand to newer arrivals on the market and a varied range of substitutes for favorite foods from cheese to bacon, ground beef to hot dogs.

Unsure about which brands to try? It can be fun to do a Web search for reviews of healthy products and see what people say. A colleague e-mailed me that she did a search for "soy ice cream" and found "VeganBlog" (blog comes from "Web log," an online diary), which offered reviews of several different flavors and brands. "I liked the fact that Soy Delicious is all organic," she wrote, "and since the reviewer noted that he/she was 'in love with' their Mint Marble Fudge, I'm going to try some." (Note: some bloggers have been known to be compensated by a product manufacturer, so you might want to take this information with a grain of salt.)

Cereals (Hot and Cold)

- Arrowhead Mills organic oatmeal
- Quaker Old Fashioned Quaker Oats or Quaker Quick Oats
- Fantastic Natural hot cereal (apple or cranberry cinnamon)
- Cheerios
- Health Valley cereals
- Nutri-Grain cereals
- Cream of Wheat
- Puffed Wheat
- Rice Chex
- Puffed Kashi cereal
- Cascadian Farms Oat & Honey Granola
- Nature's Path Organic Corn Flakes and 8 Grain Synergy Multigrain Flakes

Pancakes and Waffles

- Barbara Stitt's Pancake & Waffle Mix (also wheat-free)
- Van's Toaster Waffles (wheat-, gluten-, egg-, and yeast-free)

Bread and Crackers

- Hain's all-natural crackers
- Wheatettes reduced-fat crackers
- Hain's Rich Crackers
- Barbara's Bakery Rite Lite Rounds
- Health Valley crackers
- Wasa crackers

Grains and Snacks

- Health Valley Cheddar Lites
- Michael Season's Ultimate Crunchy Cheese Curls and Original Soy Protein Chips
- Barbara's Bakery Cheese Puffs (jalapeño and regular)

Corn Chips and Popcorn

- Unbuttered popcorn
- Bearitos corn chips

- Garden of Eatin' Little Soy Blues tortilla chips
- Garden of Eatin' natural tortilla chips

Potato/Rice/Veggie Chips
- Ray's Taro Chips
- Terra Stix
- GeniSoy crisps (Creamy Ranch, Zesty BBQ, Roasted Garlic & Onion, etc.)
- Kettle Krisps (low fat)
- Guiltless Gourmet baked chips
- Saratoga Real Vegetable Chips

Pretzels
- Newman's Own Organic Pretzels
- Oat bran pretzels
- Nabisco (fat-free) pretzels

Rice Cakes
- Hain's rice cakes
- Quaker Oat rice cakes
- Mini rice cakes

Natural Cookies
- Joseph's Sugar-Free Cookies
- Health Valley cookies (oatmeal raisin, chocolate chip, fat-free apple spice)
- Newman's Own Ginger-O's
- Country Choice certified organic wheat- and milk-free cookies (oatmeal raisin, double fudge brownies, chocolate-chip walnut)
- Country Choice certified organic vanilla wafers, ginger snaps, and bran animal cookies
- R.W. Frookie cookies

Granola and Fig Bars

- Fi-Bar all-natural snack bars
- Health Valley bars (Fat-Free Date Bakes, Fat-Free Apple Bakes, and Fat-Free Raisin Bakes)
- Health Valley granola bars
- Nature's Choice granola bars
- Fig Newmans (from Paul Newman's daughter, Nell)

Jams and Fruit Spreads

- Sorrell Ridge Spreads
- Smucker's Simply Fruit
- Polaner fruit spreads
- Knudsen's fruit spreads

Fruit Desserts

- Nature's Choice real fruit bars (the real fruit roll-ups)
- Stretch Island fruit leather, 100 percent fruit snack (Berry Blackberry, Chunk Cherry, Great Grape, and Apple)
- Dried fruits (make sure they are sulfite-free)
- Frookie Cool Fruits (frozen juice bar)
- Cherry Hill organic applesauce
- Natural Choice organic sorbet

Frozen Confections—Dairy (Organically Certified)

- Frozen yogurt bars
- Stonyfield Farms low-fat frozen yogurt ice cream

Frozen Confections—Nondairy

- Rice Dream nondairy frozen dessert (many flavors to select from)
- Fruit Stix 100 percent natural juice bars
- Tofutti Lowfat
- Tofutti Cuties (better than traditional ice cream sandwiches!)

Dairy Products (Protein)

- Organic Valley milk
- Buttermilk (all brands, low fat)
- Organic part-skim mozzarella cheese
- Low-fat ricotta cheese
- Breakstone cottage cheese (regular and snack sizes)
- Lifeway Farmer's Cheese

Nondairy Products (Protein)

- Tofutti Sour Supreme Better Than Sour Cream
- Tofutti Better Than Cream Cheese

Yogurts (Dairy and Nondairy Products) and Cheeses

- Stonyfield Farms nonfat yogurt
- Stonyfield "YoBaby" full-fat yogurt (child-size container)
- Horizon Organic yogurt
- Dannon Light 'n Fit yogurt
- Dannon Danimals snack yogurt
- Silk soy yogurt
- Whole soy yogurt
- Soyco soy cheese
- Vegan Rella (a nondairy mozzarella product)

Soy Drinks

- Whitewave's Silk soy milk (vanilla, chocolate, and eggnog for the holidays)
- Soy Dream (the least allergenic)
- WestSoy Plus soy milk
- WestSoy Lite soy milk
- WestSoy shakes (vanilla and chocolate)
- WestSoy smoothies (Banana Berry and Tropical whip)
- Pacific Foods of Oregon nondairy beverage (fortified with A, D, calcium, B vitamins, and zinc)

Nonanimal Protein Foods

- Planter's unsalted roasted peanuts
- Real Brand peanut butter (look in the dairy case)
- Smucker's all-natural peanut butter
- Pecan, almond, or cashew butter
- David Sunflower Kernels

Natural Vegetable and Fruit Juices

- After the Fall all-fruit juices (Vermont Apple, Oregon Berry, Maine Coast Blueberry, etc.)
- R.W. Knudsen (Cranberry Nectar, Papaya Nectar, Pineapple Coconut, etc.)
- Santa Cruz Organic juices
- Tomato juice (various brands)
- Vegetable juice (various brands)

Baby/Toddler Foods and Infant Formulas
for a Healthy Start

- Earth's Best organic baby foods
- Growing Healthy fresh or frozen baby food
- Organic juice
- Healthy Times Arrowroot Cookies and Cookies for Toddlers
- Gerber organic baby foods
- Beech-Nut & Gerber (with no sugar added)

Soups (Naturally Good for You)

- Pacific Foods of Oregon soups
- Walnut Acres soups
- Health Valley fat-free soups
- Chef Earl's soups

Salsa

- Pace
- Enrico's
- Muir Glen
- Seeds of Change

Natural Candy

- Panda Black licorice (high in iron, calcium, and vitamin B)
- Natural (organic) licorice twist
- Tropical Source drops (variety of flavors)
- Sunspire chocolate

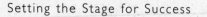

Reading Food Labels—Figuring Out What's Really in What We Eat

When you're shopping, make it a habit to read food labels and teach your children what to look for on the foods they like, especially fats, sodium, and sugars. Remind them to notice the serving size, as it may surprise them just how small a product's serving size is in relation to the nutrients it provides. Discovering that a bag of chips is supposed to provide seven or eight servings will likely come as a shock, because all the fat and sodium that's listed on that label refers to one serving only—a handful of chips!

Nutrition labels have been around for quite a while, but only in the past five years has the label provided "more complete, useful and accurate nutrition information than ever before," according to the FDA of the Department of Health and Human Services and the Food Safety and Inspection Service of the U.S. Department of Agriculture, on whose regulations the food labels are based.

In May 1999, in addition to the basics, which include calories, serving sizes, and amounts of fat, protein, and carbohydrates, the nutrition label began to supply information on the amount per serving of saturated fat, cholesterol, dietary fiber, and other important nutrients. The label also explained what percentage of a daily diet the product supplied so that consumers could understand how it fit into their overall nutrition plan.

The FDA also issued specific definitions for terms the food industry had used loosely for years—words like *light, low-fat,* and *high-fiber.* Finally, shoppers could learn how much actual juice was in a juice drink, and for some products the facts were surprising.

By November 2004, the label had gone through a number of changes, and consumers could get more detailed information than ever. Here are some definitions to help you understand the sample label provided:

Nutrition Facts

Serving Size 1 cup (228g)
Servings Per Container 2

Amount Per Serving

Calories 250	Calories from Fat 110

	% Daily Value*
Total Fat 12g	18%
Saturated Fat 3g	15%
Trans Fat 3g	
Cholesterol 30mg	10%
Sodium 470mg	20%
Total Carbohydrate 31g	10%
Dietary Fiber 0g	0%
Sugars 5g	
Protein 5g	
Vitamin A	4%
Vitamin C	2%
Calcium	20%
Iron	4%

* Percent Daily Values are based on a 2,000 calorie diet. Your Daily Values may be higher or lower depending on your calories needs

	Calories:	2,000	2,500
Total Fat	Less than	65g	80g
Sat Fat	Less than	20g	25g
Cholesterol	Less than	300mg	300mg
Sodium	Less than	2,400mg	2,400mg
Total Carbohydrate		300g	375g
Dietary Fiber		25g	30g

• *Serving Size*—This tells the size of a serving and the number of servings in a package. They're usually measured in cups or pieces, followed by the weight in grams. A package of macaroni and cheese (see sample label), for instance, contains two servings, though it may actually "serve" only one person. Two hundred and fifty calories may not seem like a lot, but five hundred for the entire entrée is one quarter of the entire day's dietary requirements.

• *Calories* and *Calories from Fat*—Calories measure how much energy you get from the food you eat. This section can be useful for managing your weight if you're counting calories or concerned about how much fat you consume. The FDA's *General Guide to Calories* says that forty calories per serving makes a food low calorie, one hundred calories is moderate, and a food that contains four hundred calories or more is high. "Calories from fat" is another useful piece of information. In this case, almost half the calories in this dish come from fat.

• *Nutrients*—This section covers nutrients that you should limit. Fats, including saturated fat and trans fat, cholesterol, and sodium have all been linked to increased risk for cardiovascular disease, high blood pressure, and some cancers. For optimum health, it's recommended that people keep their intake of saturated fat, trans fat, and cholesterol as low as possible. The lower part of this section is what the government urges Americans to "get enough of." Most people don't consume enough dietary fiber, vitamin A, vitamin C, calcium, and iron. Eating more of these nutrients can help reduce your risk of diseases like osteoporosis (calcium) and heart disease (fiber). This dish of macaroni and cheese provides a nice amount of calcium per serving, but that's offset by the amount of fat and sodium it contains.

• *Footnote and % Daily Values*—This section provides several useful pieces of nutritional information. First, it tells you the number of grams of each nutrient you should consume each day as part of a two-thousand or twenty-five-hundred calorie diet. Referring to the fat section above, you can see that one serving, half of this entrée, provides 18 percent of your "daily value" of fat grams. If you eat the entire thing, you'll be consuming twice that, or nearly 40 percent of your daily fat need. The label sets as a goal for you to eat "less than 65 grams" of fat each day, though a majority of Americans consume far more.

The sample label shows that a serving provides 10 percent of the maximum amount of cholesterol you should consume, 20 percent of a day's sodium, and about 10 percent of your day's carbohydrate allotment, though not a single gram of fiber! The FDA provides these general guidelines for % Daily Value: 5 percent or less is considered "low" and 20 percent or more is "high." Thus, you can determine that this dish is high in calcium and sodium and low in fiber, vitamins A and C, and iron.

The % Daily Value allows you to compare one product to another in a variety of nutrient categories as well as serving sizes. (Check the weight!) It also helps you understand the actual fat content of a food product, no matter what claims are made on the package (reduced fat, lite, low). Finally, you can refer to the % Daily Values to juggle what you choose to eat in a given day. This way, you don't have to give up a favorite food forever but can choose to eat it in a planned amount and on a day when you balance the rest of what you consume. If you knew, for instance, that you would be serving your dinner guests a rich ice cream that you would find hard to resist, you could decide to enjoy a half cup serving as long as the rest of that day you chose foods that were especially low in calories, fat, and sugar.

You'll note that it says "less than" a specific gram amount for fat, saturated fat, cholesterol, and sodium. However, for carbohydrates and fiber, you're advised to consume "at least" the number of grams listed—at least three hundred grams of carbohydrates daily and at least twenty-five grams of fiber.

Also, there is no % Daily Value for trans fats, sugars, and proteins on the sample label. None has been established for trans fats, which have been linked to raising LDL (the "bad" cholesterol), which may increase your risk of heart disease. No daily value has been established for sugars, which include naturally occurring sugars like those in milk and fruits, in addition to those added to a product. The same is true for protein, about which the FDA says, "Current scientific evidence indicates that protein intake is not a public health concern for adults and children over four years of age."

WHERE'S THE SUGAR?

There are many names for sugar in commercially produced foods, and it's useful to know them when you check a product's ingredient list. Ingredients are listed in descending order of weight, so if you're looking to avoid high-sugar foods, be sure that no form of sugar is one of the first few ingredients. "Disguises" for added sugar include corn syrup, high-fructose corn syrup, fruit juice concentrate, maltose, dextrose, sucrose, honey, and maple syrup.

What Do Those Labels Really Mean?

Would you like to know what the FDA means when they allow food producers to label their products "lite" or "light," "reduced," "low," or "free" when describing the amount of fat or sodium in a product?

Fat	
Fat-free	Less than 0.5 g fat per serving
Low saturated fat	1 g or less per serving
Low fat	3 g or less per serving
Reduced fat	At least 25% less fat than regular version
Light in fat	Half the fat (or less) of regular version
Sodium	
Sodium-free or salt-free	Less than 5 mg sodium per serving
Very low sodium	35 mg or less per serving
Low sodium	140 mg or less per serving
Low-sodium meal	140 mg or less per serving
Reduced or less sodium	At least 25% less sodium than regular version
Light in sodium	At least 50% less sodium than regular version
Unsalted or no salt added	No salt added during processing

Putting It All into Action

Just like in our school, you can find many opportunities to teach and model good nutritional habits. Sometimes it starts with just one small change, like turning off the television during mealtime so you can eat in a relaxed atmosphere or going on an outing to the local farmers' market. No matter where you live, what your circumstances, you can always discover ways to make the changes that last a lifetime.

This is a healthy school. It has changed my life because I have stopped eating a lot of candy and my teeth are better. I will get diabetes if I eat too much candy. You should not eat candy. You should eat vegetables and fruit. I would like to exercise more because I can lose weight. You should be a healthy person. Exercise, eat vegetables, and eat fruit.

I read labels now and explain them to my family.

—*Lauren, third grade*

The Family That Eats Together . . . Gets Healthy!

Imagine this cozy scene: parents and children seated around the dining room table, eating a homemade meal, and sharing the news of the day. Is this scenario only a fantasy at your house? For far too many Americans, shared family mealtimes are a rare occurrence. Instead, everyone grabs what's convenient, whether it means popping a frozen entrée into the microwave or picking up a couple of slices of pizza or some Chinese food on the way home.

You don't have to sit down together in order to eat healthy, but research indicates that it can really help children and adults to plan regular mealtimes and stick to them. Remember, though, it doesn't have to be all or nothing. If you can schedule a family dinner at least a couple of nights a week, you'll be making a great start!

How to make it happen? Put it on the calendar, write it in your children's homework notebooks, and do your best to say no to anything that will force you to cancel.

What makes family meals special? Here are a few things to keep in mind:

• Sit at the table together. It's just not the same if you all sit in front of the TV and eat off tray tables.

• While we're on the subject, why not let the only sound in the room be your voices talking to each other? A little soft background music would be okay, but keep the TV and video games for after dinner.

• Eat slowly and enjoy relaxed conversation. Try to encourage all of your children to stick around for at least a half hour. It takes twenty minutes minimum for your stomach to realize that you've eaten and you're satisfied, so consider serving your meal in courses: offer a salad or appetizer first, then the main event.

• Share responsibility for your family meal. Get the kids involved in whatever way you can, whether it means choosing recipes, helping with food preparation, setting and decorating the table, or serving dessert.

• Encourage participation in dinner-table conversation by inviting each family member to share a brief story, an interesting bit of news, a clever joke, or a poem. It's a great, low-risk way for children to practice speaking aloud to a group.

• Nutritionists recommend eating three meals a day and a couple of planned snacks so that we never let ourselves get too hungry or too susceptible to temptation. Teach your children that mealtimes make sense, and they're more likely to eat just what their bodies need instead of overdoing it.

EAT FAST, GET FAT?

"As a nutritionist, I can say that the slower you eat, the less likely you are to be overweight and you'll have less stress," says Linda Godfrey, child nutrition program coordinator for the Shelby County, Alabama, school system.

Remind your kids that wherever they're eating, they should try to choose carefully what they're going to eat, consume it as slowly as possible, and, as grandma used to say, CHEW that food well!

Using All Your Senses to Experience Food

By increasing your children's awareness of what they eat, you'll be teaching them to be aware of what foods they eat for the rest of their lives. Nutritionists say this is one of the most valuable tools for consuming healthy portions of good-for-us foods—simply noticing what goes into our mouths!

Just as the teachers at Browns Mill find every opportunity, no matter what the class, to teach about nutrition, you can work with your children at home to turn every meal into a journey of discovery.

1. Put away the big box of crayons and instead check out the colors of the foods we eat. Are all the oranges the same shade of orange? How about bananas? What colors correspond to the sweetest taste? Try different types of foods based on their colors.

2. Announce that dinner on a particular night will feature only foods in a particular color, and then ask the children to list all the foods they can think of in that hue. Work with them to create a menu that turns your dinner table into a palette of luscious yellows or rich reds. How close can you come to creating a healthy, well-balanced meal that is your child's favorite color?

3. Invite the family to explore the power of our sense of smell. For a fascinating and fun-filled weekend lunch, have the children make and decorate special "tasting blindfolds" out of construction paper or cardboard. Then, serve a series of foods in separate bowls and have them use their sense of smell to identify them without looking. Once they've made their guesses, continue by tasting each food. You'll probably be amazed by how the children focus on each food as they never have before.

4. Set out the ingredients for a meal that you will prepare together. Have the children notice the colors, textures, and scents of different food items, both before they are cooked and after they are ready for the table. You can even have a mini science discussion about the effects of heat on various foods. Which foods get crisp and which don't? What effect do spices have on the smell or flavor of a food? Which foods release moisture when they are cooked?

Dining Around the World

We live in an increasingly diverse culture, and it's important that the notion of America as a melting pot not just be a social studies notion. I've always taught my students that the more we know about our fellow citizens, especially their heritage and customs, the better prepared we will be to work side by side with them to ensure a peaceful world for future generations.

I also make the point that learning about others through their foods can be a lot of fun! Many schools invite parents and other family members to bring traditional foods to school on special occasions and holidays; if your child's school doesn't yet offer such an event, why not suggest it to the PTA? In the meantime, it's a great way to make mealtimes at home more exciting for everyone.

1. Try foods from other lands. You can wander the cookbook aisle at a local bookstore or library together or find good ideas on the Internet.

2. Many cultures eat far more vegetable-based dishes and less meat than Americans do. Why not increase the number of meatless meals at the same time you add dishes from other cultures to your menu? Recent studies suggest that Asian and Mediterranean countries are great sources for lively, healthy entrées that don't depend on meat.

3. Talk with your children about what they like or dislike about these new foods. Discuss the unusual ingredients in food from other cultures.

4. Visit ethnic restaurants and talk about what you see, smell, and taste. Ask, "How does a spice like lemongrass make Thai noodles different than the kind you've tried in a Chinese restaurant? Are some vegetables more commonly used in some cultures and not others? Do some cultures eat very few vegetables or only starchy ones? Is it difficult for people living here but eating foods from other countries to find the ingredients they need?"

5. Visit international markets if you have the opportunity. Talk about a wonderful way to make geography and social studies come alive for students!

6. Research your own family food heritage as a family. Ask grandparents about dishes they enjoyed as children that may no longer be on the menu. Encourage your child to make maps and perhaps even do a report for his or her class on special family food traditions that have been handed down from generation to generation. And don't be afraid to talk about whether certain dishes are healthy enough to be part of our everyday meals or whether they are best saved for special occasions only because they're high in sugar or fat, for example.

I feel great about being sugar-free! I have been going to Browns Mill for four years and ever since I've been sugar-free, I've woken up with a lot more energy. Being sugar-free has changed my life because I'm not jumping off the walls at school. I am going to be sugar-free for the rest of my life.

—*Myia, 2nd grade*

Eating Well for a Lifetime 6

Practical Advice, Ideas, and
"Recipes That Rock"
(Or So the Kids Say!)

Breakfast

Recent studies suggest that far too many school-aged children report that they skip breakfast. If your children don't eat breakfast at school, brainstorm with them about ways to make breakfast more delicious and fun—from fruit-bowl "sundaes" with fruit sauces and yogurt "whipped cream" to new ways to enjoy healthy cereals as toppings, in blends, and even in baked concoctions!

My students sign a pledge to eat a healthy breakfast that consists of carbohydrates and proteins, the combination that provides the right kind of fuel they need to succeed in school. But what does that mean?

Healthy proteins for breakfast may include eggs, which means whole eggs, egg whites, Egg Beaters or other egg substitutes; healthy breakfast meats like turkey bacon or turkey ham; veggie sausages; and low-fat cheeses (part-skim-milk cheeses like Jarlsberg are good choices).

Healthy carbohydrates include whole grains such as oatmeal,

hot and cold cereals with no sugar added, and whole-grain breads. (For best results, choose low-fat cream cheese and low-sugar fruit spreads instead of butter or margarine.) You'll also want to include fruits—fresh, frozen, or canned in unsweetened juice—and 100 percent fruit juices.

Morning No-Nos

It's a crime, really—children's bodies are being gradually destroyed all over America because kids are starting their days with foods that contain excessive amounts of sugar and fat. Check the school menus where you live to see if they're offering healthier versions of these favorites, and if they aren't, turn to chapter 9 for ideas about how to get that changed!

Healthy Kids, Smart Kids don't eat:

Doughnuts—they're fried and sugary
Muffins—the traditional high-fat kind
Sugary Cereals—especially those that come in bright, artificial
  colors!
Fried Food— pork sausages, bacon, fried egg dishes

• • • • • • • • • • • • • • • • • • • •

Sample Browns Mill breakfast menus include:

- Wheat waffles, cinnamon bagel, fresh fruit
- Veggie omelet, apple muffin, fresh fruit or juice
- English muffin with egg and cheese, baked potatoes, fresh fruit

All are served with a choice of milk, of course.

• • • • • • • • • • • • • • • • • • • •

REDUCED-SUGAR CEREALS—ARE THEY REALLY AN IMPROVEMENT?

First, food industry giant Kellogg's offered consumers their favorite brands, Frosted Flakes and Froot Loops, in a reduced-sugar version, from three teaspoons per serving to two in Frosted Flakes and from 3.75 to 2.5 in Froot Loops; then General Mills offered reduced-sugar versions of three of its most popular kids' cereals: reduced-sugar Trix, Cinnamon Toast Crunch, and Cocoa Puffs, which were developed using a blend of sugar and Splenda brand sweetener. What's next? Companies may update popular brands with more whole-grain and fiber content in response to the new dietary guidelines. Experts point out that these products still contain much more sugar than children should be consuming at breakfast, but some consider it a step in the right direction.

*News Flash! Recently, experts were asked to review the lower sugar brands of six major cereal-makers. The result: "No significant nutritional advantage over the full-sugar versions." It turns out that manufacturers replaced the sugar with other "refined carbohydrates" to "preserve the crunch." Your best bet is to feed your children cereals that are as close to unsweetened as possible—and use natural sweeteners such as berries or stewed fruits to sweeten them.

Top Ten Breakfast Treats

BLUEBERRY BERRY CRUNCHY SMOOTHIE   *Serves 2*

Berries are oh so good for you—full of healthy nutrients—that you'll probably want to make this a regular on your family menu plan. You can use thawed blueberries if you can't get fresh, but make sure that you drain them well!

This smoothie is a great breakfast on the run, but for a heartier weekend meal, use it as a starter followed by a poached egg on rye toast.

¾ cup vanilla soy milk, chilled

½ cup crushed ice

¼ cup plain low-fat yogurt

¼ cup blueberries

1 tablespoon natural granola

2 teaspoons natural sugar

1 teaspoon vanilla extract

Place ingredients in blender and blend until smooth.

Per serving: Calories: 121; Protein: 5 g; Carb: 20 g; Sugar: 13 g; Fiber: 1 g; Fat: 3 g; Sodium: 77 mg

VANILLA BANANA SMOOTHIE   *Serves 2*

I don't use the word *luscious* unless something really deserves it, and this supershake really does! Use really ripe bananas for the sweetest natural flavor.

This smoothie is all that you need to start your day with a bang!

¾ cup vanilla soy milk, chilled

½ cup crushed ice

¼ cup plain low-fat yogurt

½ cup mashed banana

2 teaspoons natural sugar

1 teaspoon vanilla extract

⅓ cup wheat germ

Place ingredients in blender and blend until smooth.

Per serving: Calories: 189; Protein: 10 g; Carb: 31 g; Sugar: 18 g; Fiber: 3 g; Fat: 4 g; Sodium: 59 mg

EGG-CITING CHEESE BREAKFAST PITA POCKET *Serves 2*

Any breakfast you can hold in your hand as you dash for the bus or the train is a winner, don't you agree? For all those middle graders and high school students who insist that they don't have time for breakfast, this is a no-brainer!

Serve with fresh sliced oranges and chilled soy milk for a great breakfast start.

2 eggs

½ teaspoon Mrs. Dash

½ teaspoon white pepper

Vegetable oil spray, such as Pam

1 ounce low-fat or soy cheese

2 small whole-grain pita pockets,
   cut in half and warmed

In a small bowl, combine eggs, salt, and pepper. Beat until well blended. Set aside. Spray small skillet or pan with cooking spray and heat over medium-high until hot, or when a bead of water bounces off the surface. Pour egg mixture into skillet and scramble eggs until done. Stir in cheese to blend. Remove the egg and cheese mixture with a spoon and place inside warmed pita halves.

Per serving: Calories: 190; Protein: 13 g; Carb: 17 g; Sugar: 1 g; Fiber: 2 g; Fat: 9 g; Sodium: 297 mg

BREAKFAST VEGGIE OMELET   *Serves 2*

I love a lot of color on my plate, especially in the morning when I need a "wake me up"! You can cut up the peppers the night before, and you'll be ready to fix this when the sun comes up!

Serve with whole-grain toast and chilled apple juice for a complete breakfast that really gets your morning off to a great start.

4 large eggs, preferably organic

½ teaspoon Mrs. Dash or Vegesal

½ teaspoon black or red pepper

Vegetable oil spray, such as Pam

1 small tomato, finely chopped

½ cup diced red bell pepper

½ cup diced green bell pepper

In a medium bowl, beat eggs with seasoning and pepper until all the white disappears. Set aside. Heat soy margarine or cooking spray in large saucepan or skillet over medium heat. Sauté tomatoes and bell peppers until lightly browned. Remove from skillet and set aside in a bowl. If needed, add another teaspoon of soy margarine or respray hot skillet. Pour egg mixture into skillet and cook without stirring for two minutes, until egg begins to ruffle up around the side of the skillet. Sprinkle sautéed vegetables to cover one half of the egg, then fold the other half over the vegetables. Carefully flip the omelet over and cook for about one minute more. Divide onto two warm plates and serve immediately.

Per serving: Calories: 190; Protein: 14 g; Carb: 8 g; Sugar: 4 g; Fiber: 2 g; Fat: 12 g; Sodium: 132 mg

FRUITY BREAKFAST SALAD   *Serves 10 (½ cup)*

This is a wonderful fruity salad that looks and tastes so good your kids won't notice how many servings of healthy fruit they're getting!

On its own, it's a terrific snack, but serve with whole-wheat toast topped with a tablespoon of natural peanut butter or slice of cheese for a complete morning meal.

I cup fresh pineapple, peeled, cored, and cubed

I cup melon, chunked

I cup strawberries, sliced

I cup plums, pitted and diced

I cup canned mandarin oranges, drained

½ cup fresh unsweetened shredded coconut

I tablespoon orange-blossom honey

Combine all fruit in a large bowl. Toss and allow to sit for 10 minutes. Sprinkle coconut over fruit. Drizzle honey over mixture.

Per serving: Calories: 57; Protein: I g; Carb: II g; Sugar: 9 g; Fiber: I.5 g; Fat: 2 g; Sodium: 4 mg

OATY PANCAKES   *Yield: 6 pancakes*

Pancakes make breakfast feel like a special occasion, and this is such an easy treat to offer your family. If you like, you could "bag up" a couple of sets of the dry ingredients to save a few morning minutes.

Serve pancakes with a poached egg and chilled vanilla soy milk to ensure that you have a hearty well-balanced breakfast.

½ cup oat flour

½ cup all-purpose flour

1 teaspoon baking powder

1 teaspoon baking soda

1 large egg

1 cup soy milk

½ cup fresh strawberries, sliced

Preheat griddle or skillet over moderate heat. Lightly coat with cooking spray. In a medium bowl, combine all dry ingredients and set aside. Beat egg and add milk, mixing well. Slowly add egg mixture to flour mixture and beat until smooth. Using ⅓ cup mixture for each pancake, cook until bubbles appear on the surface, about 1 minute. Turn gently and brown flip side. Keep pancakes in warm oven until all are cooked. Garnish with strawberries and serve.

Per pancake: Calories: 95; Protein: 4 g; Carb: 14 g; Sugar: 1 g; Fiber: 2 g; Fat: 3 g; Sodium: 292 mg

SENSATIONAL APPLESAUCE   *Serves 4 (½ cup)*

We loved it when we were babies, and we still get a lot of pleasure at the idea of homemade applesauce. I love to stir up a batch after a visit to a local orchard every fall.

Serve this applesauce with whole-grain bread topped with low-fat cheese and a glass of chilled 100 percent grape juice.

2 large red apples   1 teaspoon allspice
1 cup water

Preheat oven to 350 degrees. Wash apples and place in a small baking pan. Pour in water. Bake for 30 minutes and remove from oven. Remove apples from the pan and allow to cool. When cool enough to handle, remove skins and core. Mash apples until they are the consistency you like, add allspice, and stir until fully blended.

Per serving: Calories: 64; Protein: 0 g; Carb: 17 g; Sugar: 13 g; Fiber: 3 g; Fat: 0 g; Sodium: 2 mg

BASIC BLUEBERRY MUFFINS

Yield: 12 muffins

Because they are so good for us, the more berries we can eat, the better, so buy them when they're in season and freeze a few pints for later.

Serve these muffins with a low-fat cream cheese and some 100 percent fruit juice for a scrumptious combination—and a nutritious breakfast!

2 cups all-purpose flour

½ cup natural sugar

1½ teaspoons baking powder

½ teaspoon baking soda

1 cup fresh, washed, and dried, or
   frozen, blueberries

2 large eggs, preferably organic

1 cup soy milk

⅓ cup vegetable oil

1 teaspoon vanilla extract

Preheat oven to 400 degrees. Into a medium bowl, sift flour, sugar, baking powder, and baking soda together. Stir to blend. Add blueberries and toss to coat. In a small bowl, combine eggs, milk, oil, and vanilla extract. Gradually add the egg mixture to the flour mixture and stir gently until batter is smooth. Pour batter into lightly greased 12-cup muffin pan, filling each cup ⅔ full with batter. Bake for 20 minutes, until lightly browned.

Per muffin: Calories: 195; Protein: 4 g; Carb: 27 g; Sugar: 10 g; Fiber: 1 g; Fat: 8 g; Sodium: 116 mg

APPLE SPICE OATMEAL   *Serves 6*

This is a wonderfully fragrant version of one of the best choices for a healthy breakfast. Not only do oats help lower cholesterol, but this dish is a real kid pleaser!

Serve oatmeal with skim or soy milk and sprinkle with cinnamon, if you wish. Add fresh orange slices on the side for a good start to the day.

3½ cups water   1 teaspoon cinnamon
½ cup apple, chopped   Honey
2 cups old-fashioned oats

Bring water to a boil in a heavy saucepan over medium heat. Add the chopped apple and cook for 2 minutes. Slowly stir in the oats and cinnamon and bring back to a boil. Turn heat down to medium low and cook for 5 minutes, stirring occasionally. Remove from heat and allow to cool for several minutes. Serve with a drizzle of honey or scoop of applesauce (see recipe page 118).

Per serving: Calories: 106; Protein: 4 g; Carb: 20 g; Sugar: 2 g; Fiber: 3 g; Fat: 2 g; Sodium: 4 mg

Lunch

A terrific lunch may begin with a vegetable-based soup—homemade or from one of the many healthful store brands. Look for soups that feature beans for a great protein boost and lots of healthy fiber. Sandwiches on whole grain bread satisfy the appetite, especially when they are filled with lean meats, vegetarian spreads like hummus and baba ghanoush, canned fish (tuna, salmon), or natural peanut butter. Fruit provides a sweet finish to this midday meal, and you can delight your children with home-baked apples topped with light maple syrup and cinnamon. (Great warm or cold!) And of course salads filled with all kinds of crunchy and colorful vegetables please the eye and the palate. If you're packing lunch, send a low-fat dressing in a separate container.

Sampling of the Browns Mill lunch menu:

- Baked chicken on a wheat roll, mashed potatoes, green beans, fresh fruit
- Baked fish, cornbread, black-eyed peas, steamed sweet potatoes, seasoned greens
- Veggie pizza, whole kernel corn, mixed green salad, banana

My Brown-Bag Essentials

I hope that someday soon all school kitchens will serve healthier and more nutritious meals to all students everywhere. In the meantime, your children's best bet at lunch may be carried to school in a brown bag that *you* pack. When you give your children the nutritional fuel their bodies require, they'll have the necessary energy and focus to do what they want and need to do. Every brown bag should include these essentials:

Protein: Chicken salad, egg salad, and peanut butter are all great choices for sandwich fillings. For more adventurous palates, experiment with a flavorful soy or tofu burger. You'll find a variety of flavors in your grocer's freezer. Nuts are also an excellent protein source for children. Why not make your own trail mix with nuts and dried fruits?

Grain: Whole-wheat bread is a great choice for sandwiches. Other good sources are crackers, rice cakes, natural grain bagels, animal crackers, granola bars, veggie chips, tortillas, and popcorn.

Fruit: For a high-energy charge, a handful of grapes, a dish of strawberries, or a ripe banana just might do the trick. Send natural fruit juices in small containers that you freeze overnight. Place them in zippered plastic bags so they can thaw and provide a nicely chilled drink at lunchtime. Also get children to eat fruit by using fruit spreads or full-fruit jams on peanut-butter sandwiches or bagels.

Vegetables: They come in all shapes and textures, and they're filling, too! Veggie sticks—celery, carrots—or cherry/grape tomatoes are a healthy addition to a bagged lunch. A small can of vegetable juice is another way to deliver lots of good-for-you nutrients.

Dairy or soy: These round out a brown-bag lunch by delivering a feeling of satisfaction and fullness. Good sources of dairy and soy include yogurt and low-fat cheeses. Both appeal to children and are recommended additions.

These brown-bag essentials are not just for kids. A business executive who chooses to dine in will have a more energetic afternoon with a lunch that follows these common-sense "rules." Anytime you're on the run, out and about having fun, or juggling carpools and kids' activities, you'll find that a well-packed brown-bag meal will keep you well nourished and out of fast-food restaurants whose menus overflow with high-fat, high-sugar, overly processed foods. The key to a healthy lifestyle—one you can live with for a lifetime— might be "hidden" inside a plain little brown bag!

THE LUNCH "HOUR"

I recently read in the *Birmingham* (Alabama) *News* that students in most Birmingham area schools get less than thirty minutes for lunch, which gives new meaning to the expression "eat and run." It's not surprising that some children skip their meals while others gobble down their food double-time. The article went on to say that although the Alabama Department of Education "recommends" students have at least thirty minutes to eat lunch, most schools allot just twenty to twenty-eight minutes per lunch period.

Dr. Frank Franklin, professor of pediatrics and nutrition science at the University of Alabama at Birmingham, expressed his concern. "When you're given limited time, you're going to go for the food that is fast like pizza, chocolate chip cookies, corn, and chicken nuggets," he said. "Some of that stuff you can eat without even chewing it. All it is is fat and sugar."

Linda Godfrey, child nutrition program coordinator for the Shelby County (Alabama) school system, says, "From a scheduling standpoint, it's difficult to incorporate that much time into the day because there's so much pressure on educators for academics. But all the education in the world doesn't mean anything if you're unhealthy."

What's the answer? Dr. Franklin suggests an extra fifteen to twenty minutes be added to the school day, but for most schools, that may not be possible.

What these experts say is true: eating in a hurry, grabbing food on the run, *can* lead to eating and overeating all the wrong foods . But it doesn't *have* to if your children's school provides only healthy choices!

Ten Terrific Homemade Lunches

TURKEY BURGER ON RYE   *Yield: 4 patties*

Served on rye or wheat bread, this makes an excellent alternative to a higher fat beef burger, even for a family of confirmed beef lovers.

Dress this quarter-pounder with mild purple onion, slices of tomato, red leaf lettuce, and whatever condiments you prefer. Note that ketchup is often high in sugar, so use it sparingly.

I pound ground turkey	I teaspoon red pepper
I teaspoon Mrs. Dash	I teaspoon garlic powder

In a medium bowl, mix the ground turkey with salt, pepper, and garlic powder. Divide and shape into four burgers. Heat skillet over medium heat and cook burgers on one side for about 4 minutes. Flip and cook until done, about another 4 minutes.

Per serving, plain burger: Calories: 231; Protein: 18 g; Carb: 2 g; Sugar: 0 g; Fiber: 0 g; Fat: 17 g; Sodium: 117 mg

Per serving, burger with 2 slices of rye bread: Calories: 397; Protein: 24 g; Carb: 33 g; Sugar: 5 g; Fiber: 4 g; Fat: 19 g; Sodium: 540 mg

ALL-AMERICAN SUB SANDWICH   *Serves 2*

Why choose red leaf lettuce over iceberg or romaine? It's colorful, it tastes really good, and it's more nutritious.

Serve with fresh Roman apple slices instead of the standard potato chips and 100 percent fruit juice of your choice.

1 (12-inch) piece of oat, rye, or wheat sub sandwich bread cut in half

2 teaspoons low-fat Nayonnaise or other low-calorie, low-fat mayonnaise

1 teaspoon yellow mustard

Red or green leaf lettuce

4 slices tomato

4 slices red or white onion

4 ounces reduced-salt sliced turkey or chicken

Cut the sub loaf in half lengthwise. Spread with Nayonnaise and mustard. Layer with red leaf lettuce, tomato, onion, and turkey or chicken. Cut in half crosswise.

Per serving: Calories: 282; Protein: 19 g; Carb: 44 g; Sugar: 7 g; Fiber: 4 g; Fat: 4 g; Sodium: 746 mg

TASTY TACO SALAD   *Serves 6*

Some Mexican-style dishes are high in fat, but not this festive dish made with healthy ground turkey and lots of crunchy onions. I like mine with tangy salsa on top!

You can make this dish "portable" by packing individual portions of the meat, veggies, and chips (and cheese, if you choose) in separate compartments of a plastic container and carried in a cooler to school where it can be easily assembled. Serve with purple plums and 100 percent fruit juice for a nutritious change from sandwiches.

I pound ground turkey	9 ounces natural taco chips
½ cup chopped onions	I head green lettuce, shredded
½ teaspoon sea salt	I tomato, chopped
½ teaspoon black pepper	

In a heavy, medium skillet, cook the turkey with the onion, salt, and pepper until turkey is browned. Drain well. Spread the taco chips on a plate and cover with ground turkey. Place lettuce and tomatoes on top of turkey. If desired, top with shredded low-fat cheese or soy cheese and serve.

Per serving: Calories: 387; Protein: 16 g; Carb: 29 g; Sugar: 1 g; Fiber: 3 g; Fat: 22 g; Sodium: 429 mg

SPECTACULAR SPINACH WRAP   *Serves 4*

When you're tired of the same old, same old, surprise your mouth with this fruity, nutty, tangy sandwich. You'll be glad you did!

Serve with fresh pear slices and chilled 100 percent grape juice for a lunch that won't leave you feeling sluggish all afternoon!

8 ounces fresh spinach	¼ cup chopped pecans
½ purple onion, sliced	⅓ cup low-fat ranch dressing
1 cup sliced strawberries	4 (10-inch) low-fat flour tortillas

Remove stems and wash spinach in cold water. Wrap the spinach in paper towels and squeeze out all the excess water. In a medium bowl toss the spinach with the onion, strawberries, pecans, and salad dressing. Spoon a quarter of the mixture onto each of the four tortillas and wrap tightly, being sure to tuck in the ends as you go.

Per serving: Calories: 285; Protein: 6 g; Carb: 31 g; Sugar: 5 g; Fiber: 4 g; Fat: 16 g; Sodium: 645 mg

PIZZA POCKET   *Serves 1*

Trade in the traditional high-fat pepperoni for this tasty turkey sausage, and your passion for pizza will be truly satisfied! There are many good choices in pasta sauce, so read the ingredients and find one you like best.

To "brown-bag," wrap these tightly in foil and Saran wrap or place in a resealable plastic bag or plastic container. Serve with red grapes and plain low-fat yogurt for a filling and energizing lunch.

2 ounces turkey sausage, thinly   ¼ cup shredded reduced-fat
   sliced   mozzarella cheese
1 pita pocket
2 tablespoons low-sodium pasta
   sauce, preferably organic

Preheat oven to 350 degrees. Brown sliced sausage lightly on both sides. Cut pita in half crosswise and spoon pasta sauce into each half. Add sausage and cheese. Place the sandwich halves on a baking sheet and bake for 3 to 5 minutes or until cheese melts.

Per serving: Calories: 335; Protein: 23 g; Carb: 39 g; Sugar: 2 g; Fiber: 5 g; Fat: 12 g; Sodium: 889 mg

EGG-CELLENT CURRY SALAD SANDWICH   *Serves 8*

Just when you thought an egg salad sandwich couldn't get any better—
or better for you—here's a savory version that will wake up your taste
buds.

Serve with a side of Red Delicious apple slices.

8 large eggs, preferably organic

½ cup dill relish

2 tablespoons finely chopped onion

½ teaspoon sea salt

½ teaspoon cayenne or black
  pepper

½ teaspoon curry powder

2 tablespoons Nayonnaise or low-
  calorie, low-sodium mayonnaise

1 teaspoon mustard

16 slices oat bread (also good with
  wheat and sourdough)

8 leaves romaine lettuce

Hard-boil eggs by gently placing in boiling water and cooking for 15
minutes. Remove from heat, drain, and fill pot with cold water, letting
eggs cool until you are able to handle them to peel. In a medium bowl,
coarsely chop eggs. Stir in the relish, onion, salt, pepper, curry powder,
and Nayonnaise, mixing as you go until well blended.

   Assemble the sandwiches with the bread and lettuce. There's no
need for extra butter or margarine since this salad is nice and creamy.

Per serving, egg salad: Calories: 100; Protein: 7 g; Carb: 5 g; Sugar: 3 g; Fiber: 0 g;
Fat: 6 g; Sodium: 298 mg

Per serving, egg salad with bread: Calories: 231; Protein: 12 g; Carb: 29 g; Sugar: 6 g;
Fiber: 4 g; Fat: 8 g; Sodium: 552 mg

CHICKEN SALAD SURPRISE   *Serves 8*

This fruity chicken salad is surprisingly good—and surprisingly fun to eat. Doesn't everyone love a surprise?

Serve with a slice of rye or wheat bread, plain or toasted, and honeydew melon for a great lunch.

4 cups (20 ounces) shredded, chopped, cooked chicken

½ cup diced, peeled Red Delicious apple

1 cup red seedless grapes, chopped

½ cup onion, finely chopped

½ cup low-fat Nayonnaise or low-fat natural mayonnaise

½ teaspoon cayenne pepper

½ teaspoon sea salt

Combine chicken, apple, and grapes. Toss and let stand for 3 minutes. Add remaining ingredients to chicken mixture and toss until well mixed. Cover and refrigerate until chilled.

Per serving: Calories: 216; Protein: 18 g; Carb: 9 g; Sugar: 5 g; Fiber: 1 g; Fat: 12 g; Sodium: 398 mg

1-2-3 VEGGIE SOUP   *Serves 6*

If you thought you needed hours to make a delicious homemade vegetable soup, I'm happy to show you a new way to get your veggies—
fast! If you like your soup extratangy, look for cans of diced tomatoes
that have chilis or jalapenos already mixed in!

*This is a perfect "thermos" lunch that goes great with Saucy Veggie Corn-
bread Cakes (page 132). Finish lunch with fresh cubed pineapple as a
sweet and healthy treat.*

2 cups water

1 (16-ounce) bag frozen mixed
  vegetables

1 (12-ounce) can low-sodium diced
  tomatoes (with chilis or
  jalapenos, optional)

⅓ cup tomato paste

2 teaspoons Vegesal or Mrs. Dash

1 teaspoon sea salt

½ teaspoon black pepper

In a large, heavy pot, bring the water to a boil over medium-high heat.
Add vegetables, tomatoes, and tomato paste. Add seasonings and stir.
Bring back to a boil. Reduce heat to low and simmer for 30 minutes,
stirring occasionally.

Per serving: Calories: 71; Protein: 3 g; Carb: 16 g; Sugar: 6 g; Fiber: 4 g; Fat: 0 g;
Sodium: 500 mg

SAUCY VEGGIE CORNBREAD CAKES   *Yield: 6 cakes*

We really enjoy our cornbread here in the South, but even if you're not in the habit of serving it, these flavorful cakes will win you over.

Serve with the 1-2-3 Veggie Soup (page 131) and chilled 100 percent grape juice for a winning lunch!

I cup natural yellow cornmeal

I teaspoon baking powder

½ teaspoon salt

½ teaspoon red pepper

½ cup green onion, chopped

½ cup tomatoes, diced

⅛ cup celery, diced

I large egg, preferably organic

½ cup soy milk

Preheat a griddle or heavy skillet over medium-high heat, and lightly coat with cooking spray when ready to cook. In a medium bowl, combine all dry ingredients and vegetables; set aside. Beat egg, and then add milk and mix well. Add egg mixture to cornmeal mixture and blend until smooth. For each cake, pour ⅓ cup mixture onto the hot griddle or skillet and cook for one minute or until bubbles appear on the surface. Turn gently and brown flip side, about 1 minute.

Per serving: Calories: 112; Protein: 4 g; Carb: 22 g; Sugar: 2 g; Fiber: 2 g; Fat: 2 g; Sodium: 309 mg

TUNA AND TOFU SALAD   *Serves 8*

Talk about a meal that's high in protein and rich in texture! The onion gives this just the right amount of crunch.

Serve on whole wheat bread, plain or toasted, and with fresh blueberries for dessert.

I (12-ounce) can tuna (in water), drained

½ cup firm tofu, chopped

½ sweet white onion, chopped

½ cup chopped dill pickles

½ cup low-fat Nayonnaise or low-fat natural mayonnaise

½ teaspoon sea salt

I teaspoon black pepper

In a medium bowl, break up tuna into flakes, add tofu, and mix well. Add onion and pickles; mix well. Add Nayonnaise, salt, and pepper, and stir. Cover and refrigerate for 30 minutes to allow flavors to blend, or serve immediately.

Per serving, salad only: Calories: 119; Protein: 11 g; Carb: 4 g; Sugar: 1 g; Fiber: 0 g; Fat: 7 g; Sodium: 559 mg

Snacks

Some parents are surprised to learn that snacking is not only good for children but almost a necessity. Why? Their stomachs are smaller, which means that they will eat less at one sitting than we might feel is enough. A child who regularly leaves a lot of food on his or her plate might do better to eat six small meals a day instead of three larger ones. Just think of it as three meals and three snacks, and it won't seem like too much work.

It's important to be prepared with healthy snacking foods. Let your kids know where to find what you want them to eat—cut-up veggies, small pieces of fresh fruit, individual containers of canned fruit, and low-fat dairy (yogurt, string cheese) in the fridge, and small plastic bags filled with measured-out quantities of baked chips, crackers, rice cakes, and healthy cookies, stored in an accessible cabinet or countertop basket.

I found a terrific piece of advice on the Web site www.diabetic-lifestyle.com, which suggested that parents offer children "comparable" snacks. Suggest, "Grapes or apple slices?" "Carrots or celery sticks?" not "Carrots or pretzels?" They also suggested keeping quantities appropriate—less food for a younger, smaller child than for an older one. I remember a professor who once said, "What's fair doesn't mean that everyone gets the same."

Be sure to offer a variety of healthy foods so that your children will develop a taste for many different snacks. Also, keep snacks age-appropriate; choking is a real concern with very young children. Nutritionists suggest parents avoid giving children younger than three nuts, raisins, popcorn, chunks of hard fruit or vegetables, sticky jelly-type foods, or hot dogs—all too easy for little ones to choke on.

Healthy Snacks to Make the Brain and Body Work

I needed delicious "ammunition" when my students and their families said, "What are we going to eat? We need snacks, fun food." It's good to talk about snacking, too. Discuss which foods satisfy which needs. So before grabbing just anything, think about what you and your kids really want:

Juicy: Choose from a variety of fruits—oranges, grapes, apples, or kiwis

Crispy or crunchy: Try pumpkin seeds, carrot sticks, cucumber strips, toast, cereal mixed with nuts, or celery sticks

Warm: Sip soup, cider, or herbal tea

To satisfy thirst: Drink vegetable juices, fruit or yogurt shakes, and lots of water

---

SMART SNACKING TIPS

• Discourage your child from snacking in front of the TV. Start now to prevent the bad habit of unconscious eating, which usually leads to overeating.

• Ask your children to help choose their own healthy snacks, so you won't hear a chorus of "There's nothing to eat around here!"

• Establish a snack schedule (after school, after evening homework) to discourage a child from "grazing" all day long.

• Offer satisfying substitutes for traditional snacks: fruit leather instead of a candy bar, a granola bar instead of cookies, or a small bagel or English muffin topped with fruit spread instead of a jelly doughnut.

Healthy Snacks Kids Enjoy

PERFECT PIZZA   *Serves 4*

If you want pizza that has plenty of pizzazz and is better for you than the kind you get delivered, this should be perfect for you! I suggest onions, peppers, and mushrooms on top, but if you love other veggies, feel free to substitute them.

2 tablespoons oil, divided	I teaspoon Vegesal
½ cup sliced onions	¼ teaspoon black pepper
½ cup sliced mushrooms	I recipe Pizza Sauce (page 137)
½ cup sliced bell peppers	4 (6-inch) whole-wheat tortillas
10 ounces ground lean turkey	I cup low-fat mozzarella cheese

Preheat oven to 350 degrees. In a medium, heavy skillet, heat 1 tablespoon of the oil over medium-high heat. Sauté onions, mushrooms, and peppers in 1 tablespoon oil until browned. Set aside. To the same skillet, add the remaining oil and cook ground turkey, seasoning with Vegesal and pepper and stirring constantly until meat is browned and crumbled. Remove from heat and drain.

Spread one quarter of the sauce over each tortilla and layer meat, then vegetable mixture. Sprinkle each pizza with cheese. Place pizza on baking sheet and cook for 5 minutes or until cheese melts.

Per serving: Calories: 390; Protein: 23 g; Carb: 33 g; Sugar: 3 g; Fiber: 5 g; Fat: 22 g; Sodium: 455 mg

PIZZA SAUCE

Yield: 4 servings (about ½ cup each)

1½ cups no-salt-added tomato
  sauce

½ cup natural diced tomato

2 teaspoons dried oregano

Place all ingredients in heavy, medium saucepan over medium heat. Bring to a boil, reduce heat to low, and simmer for 30 minutes, stirring occasionally.

Per serving: Calories: 34; Protein: 1 g; Carb: 8 g; Sugar: 1 g; Fiber: 2 g; Fat: 0 g; Sodium: 50 mg

GINGERED CARROTS AND APPLES

Serves 6

Take one naturally sweet vegetable, add one naturally sweet fruit, and blend with a little sweetener and one of my favorite spices. This also makes a nice side dish served hot.

Serve with plain soy yogurt sprinkled with ginger for dipping.

1 (16-ounce) bag baby carrots

½ cup diced red apple

½ cup water

1 tablespoon organic brown sugar

1 teaspoon ginger

Preheat oven to 350 degrees. Wash carrots and place in a medium bowl with diced apple and water. Sprinkle with brown sugar and ginger and toss until sugar and ginger are dissolved. Place mixture in an 11½" × 7" baking dish. Bake for 15 minutes or until carrots are fork tender. Remove from oven and allow to cool before serving.

Per serving: Calories: 51; Protein: 1 g; Carb: 12 g; Sugar: 8 g; Fiber: 2 g; Fat: 0 g; Sodium: 42 mg

BAKED LEMON PEPPER WINGS   *Serves 24 (2 wings each)*

This recipe makes a lot of wings, but they taste so good, they won't last very long! Your friends and family may be surprised by what a little lemon and some red pepper can do to good old chicken.

1 (48-ounce) bag chicken wings	½ teaspoon red pepper
1 large lemon	2 teaspoons Vegesal

Preheat oven to 425 degrees. Place chicken wings in a large bowl. Roll lemon back and forth to soften, and then slice in half and squeeze juice over wings. Sprinkle red pepper and Vegesal over wings and toss well. Place wings on lightly greased baking sheet with half-inch lip and bake for 25 minutes. Remove the sheet from the oven carefully, drain any liquid, and turn wings over. Return wings to oven and bake for an additional 20 minutes or until crisp. Allow to cool slightly before serving.

Per serving: Calories: 165; Protein: 15 g; Carb: 0 g; Sugar: 0 g; Fiber: 0 g; Fat: 11 g; Sodium: 47 mg

CELERY AND CRAISINS BUTTER   *Serves 4 (2 pieces each)*

When your kids aren't sure what they want to eat after school, offer them a couple of these. They satisfy lots of snacking urges, from crunchy to sweet.

3 tablespoons natural peanut
  butter or cashew butter
½ teaspoon honey

8 (4-inch long) pieces celery
½ cup Craisins (dried cranberries)

In a small bowl, cream the peanut or cashew butter and honey together. Fill celery ribs and sprinkle on Craisins. Serve immediately or chill if desired.

Per serving: Calories: 124; Protein: 3 g; Carb: 16 g; Sugar: 14 g; Fiber: 2 g; Fat: 6 g; Sodium: 63 mg

CEREAL TRAIL MIX   *Serves 8 (about ½ cup each)*

Commercial trail mix, even the organic kind, can be high in fat. Why not make your own using healthy granola and the best-tasting dried fruits and nuts you can find? Store each serving in an individual resealable plastic bag, which helps "portion control" as well as makes this snack easy to pop into a lunch bag or to grab on the go.

3 cups natural granola, unsweetened
½ cup dried fruit

½ cup chopped roasted almonds

In a large bowl, mix all ingredients together. Divide into six portions and store in individual resealable plastic bags in the refrigerator.

Per serving: Calories: 190; Protein: 4 g; Carb: 35 g; Sugar: 11 g; Fiber: 4 g; Fat: 5 g; Sodium: 85 mg

SPICY POPCORN   *Serves 10*

This is one of my favorite cooking secrets—the power of yeast flakes that give popcorn that wonderful buttery taste! And the seasoning doesn't add all the extra sodium that salt does. Invite the family for a DVD movie festival and serve bowls of this treat or pack it up for a portable snack!

½ cup popping corn   2 teaspoons yeast flakes
1 tablespoon oil (optional,   1 teaspoon Mrs. Dash seasoning
  depending on cooking method
  of popcorn)

Prepare popcorn as directed by manufacturer or in oiled Dutch oven with cover. Remove from pot and place in a medium bowl. While popcorn is still hot, add yeast flakes and seasoning and toss well. Serve immediately or let cool and store in individual resealable plastic bags.

Per serving, includes oil: Calories: 63; Protein: 2 g; Carb: 10 g; Sugar: 0 g; Fiber: 2 g; Fat: 2 g; Sodium: 1 mg

This nutrition program has affected my life in many different ways. From a sports point of view, I am faster, stronger, and more flexible. For example, I take tae kwon do, and before class we stretch. I can now stretch farther than I used to. (That's another story though.)

Healthwise, my sugar level is lower, which means I'm less hyperactive. At my last physical, my doctor said I'm doing pretty good and my blood pressure has dropped (though it is still high). At the one before that, my sugar level was high and my blood pressure was higher.

So, since I've been on the nutrition program, my health has been much better. In the past, my teeth were horrible but now they are better. I've been much healthier since I've been in the program—and that's how it has changed my life.

—*Aaron, sixth grade*

TEACHABLE MOMENTS

Tonight at dinner, why not ask family members to name their three favorite foods? Invite one child to be the "scribe" and list them on a sheet of paper. Then discuss which of them are the healthiest and which ones the family would like to eat more often. Assign an older child to research recipes for those foods on the Internet; suggest that the younger children work with you to create menus featuring those foods.

On another evening, ask family members to name foods that they have never tried but would like to. Assign a different scribe to take notes, and suggest that the children look through cookbooks or online to find out how healthy those foods are and how they might be prepared. Plan a family cooking extravaganza on a weekend afternoon that ends with a tasting "buffet" of the new dishes. Vote on which ones will make it onto your new list of family favorites!

Dinner/Supper

If you think of the dinner plate divided into quarters, design your healthy evening meal like this: one-quarter of the plate is the protein, usually lean meat, fish, or veggie; one-half of the plate is one or more vegetables; and one-quarter of the plate should contain some kind of whole-grain product—brown rice, whole-grain pasta or noodles, or a starchy potato with skin on if possible. Lots of nutrients just beneath the skin can be lost to peeling! For dessert, choose one of my recipes or select a fresh fruit salad topped with a few nuts or a fruit-based sauce, which makes it a sundae!

Beverage choices can include water, fruit or vegetable juices, and perhaps even fruit spritzers if you're so inclined—combine half juice and half sparkling/fizzy water, garnish with sliced fruit, and you'll feel as if you're at a festive dinner party! Soy milk or low-fat/fat-free milk can be selected at a meal or as part of daily snacks; nondairy ice creams and sorbets are wonderful, too.

A-Plus Anytime Dinners the Whole Family Will Love

ALMOND CHICKEN

Serves 8

It's just simple baked chicken and vegetables, but with a touch of almonds, it's a visit to a French country restaurant. Rosemary and chicken were made to be together, too!

Serve with Creamy Cauliflower and Potatoes (page 144) and steamed green beans for a memorable and healthy evening meal.

1 whole chicken (2½ lbs.)	½ pound sliced mushrooms, such
Sea salt and pepper, to taste	as Baby Bella
1 small onion, sliced	½ pound carrots, sliced to ½ inch
1 small green bell pepper, sliced	1 teaspoon rosemary
2 cloves garlic, thinly sliced	½ cup sliced almonds

Preheat oven to 350 degrees. Remove the skin. Cut into pieces—breasts, legs, thighs, and so forth. Place in a baking dish or casserole large enough so that pieces are in one layer; sprinkle with sea salt and pepper. Layer the onion and bell pepper on top and around the chicken. Add garlic, mushrooms, and carrots. Sprinkle with rosemary. Cover with foil and bake for 35 minutes. Remove from oven and sprinkle almonds on top. Return to oven uncovered and bake for 10 minutes.

Per serving: Calories: 163; Protein: 18 g; Carb: 6 g; Sugar: 2 g; Fiber: 2 g; Fat: 7 g; Sodium: 278 mg

CREAMY CAULIFLOWER AND POTATOES   *Serves 8*

Here are two vegetables that make each other better, getting more healthy veggies into your kids! Make sure you use unflavored soy milk with this recipe.

2 medium potatoes, peeled and
   diced

2 cups cauliflower florets

2 cups water, for cooking
   vegetables

1 teaspoon sea salt

½ teaspoon black pepper

¼ cup soy milk

Place the diced potatoes and cauliflower florets in a colander, rinse under cold running water, and then allow to drain. Place the vegetables in a medium, heavy saucepan, cover with water (about 2 cups), and bring to a boil over medium heat. Cook for 20 minutes or until fork tender. Remove from heat, drain, and place in a medium mixing bowl. Add salt, pepper, and soy milk. Mix well and serve hot.

Per serving: Calories: 36; Protein: 2 g; Carb: 8 g; Sugar: 1 g; Fiber: 2 g; Fat: 0 g; Sodium: 298 mg

ALL-CALL LASAGNA

Serves 12

This dish freezes beautifully, *if* you have any leftovers!
Serve with a simple tossed salad for a healthy meal.

1 (12-ounce) box regular lasagna noodles	1 tablespoon garlic, chopped
2 cups low-fat cottage cheese	1 tablespoon canola oil
1½ cups part-skim ricotta cheese	2 pounds ground turkey
2 (9-ounce) boxes frozen whole spinach, thawed	1 teaspoon black pepper
1 tablespoon soy margarine	1 teaspoon Vegesal
1 cup onion, chopped	1 (16-ounce) can low-sodium tomato sauce
	2 cups low-fat mozzarella cheese

Preheat oven to 325 degrees. Cook lasagna noodles as directed on box. While noodles are cooking, combine low-fat cottage cheese and ricotta cheese in a medium bowl. Using a paper towel or a clean, lint-free dishcloth, squeeze moisture from thawed spinach. In a small, heavy saucepan over medium heat, melt the margarine. Add onions and garlic to pan and sauté for 3 minutes. Set aside. In a large, heavy skillet, heat the oil over medium heat. Add the ground turkey, pepper, and Vegesal, and cook, stirring constantly until turkey browns and crumbles. Drain off excess liquid, then add tomato sauce, spinach, and cooked onions and garlic. Simmer over low heat for 15 minutes. Lightly coat a 13" × 9" × 2" pan with cooking spray. Layer turkey-tomato-sauce mixture, cheese mixture, mozzarella cheese (reserving ½ cup), and cooked drained lasagna noodles alternately in pan, ending with the cheese mixture. Sprinkle ½ cup of mozzarella cheese on top. Bake uncovered for approximately 45 minutes.

Per serving: Calories: 362; Protein: 26 g; Carb: 30 g; Sugar: 4 g; Fiber: 3 g; Fat: 16 g; Sodium: 343 mg

SAUCY SPAGHETTI WITH TURKEY

Serves 8

If you're like me, you enjoy finding all those bits of meat and vegetables in your spaghetti sauce! Each forkful arrives full of flavorful surprises and persuades you that you're eating a really filling dish.

Serve with steamed broccoli for a well-rounded meal.

1 (16-ounce) box thin spaghetti

2 tablespoons oil

1 small onion, chopped

1 large tomato, chopped

1 cup mushrooms, chopped

1 pound lean ground turkey

1 (16-ounce) jar (can) no-salt-added tomato sauce

1 (12-ounce) can no-salt-added tomato paste

2 cups water

2 teaspoons Vegesal

1 teaspoon oregano

½ teaspoon white pepper

Prepare spaghetti as directed on the box. While the noodles are cooking, heat the oil in a heavy, medium skillet over medium heat, and sauté vegetables for 3 minutes. Set aside. In deep, large, heavy skillet, brown meat over medium heat, stirring constantly until meat is brown and crumbled. Drain off any excess liquid. Reduce heat to medium-low, add sautéed vegetables, and stir in tomato sauce, tomato paste, water, and seasonings. Continue to cook for 20 minutes, stirring occasionally. In a large bowl, combine the sauce and the noodles to coat completely. Divide and serve on warmed plates.

Per serving: Calories: 419; Protein: 21 g; Carb: 58 g; Sugar: 5 g; Fiber: 5 g; Fat: 13 g; Sodium: 109 mg

CHICKEN LOAF SPECIAL   *Serves 8*

Meat loaf is an American tradition, no matter where in the country you hail from. This version, made with ground chicken, is a little lighter but no less satisfying.

Try this with my Squash Casserole (page 148) and a fresh green vegetable.

I large egg, preferably organic

I (14.5-ounce) can no-salt-added
   diced tomatoes

2 tablespoons no-salt-added
   tomato paste

2 pounds ground chicken

I small onion, minced

⅓ cup minced garlic

I cup crushed wheat crackers

I teaspoon Vegesal

½ teaspoon cayenne pepper

Preheat oven to 350 degrees. In small bowl, beat the egg and mix in the diced tomatoes and tomato paste. In large bowl, combine ground chicken with tomato mixture. Add remaining ingredients; mix well. Pack the mixture into an ungreased 9" × 5" × 3" loaf pan. Bake, uncovered, for 45 minutes.

Per serving: Calories: 291; Protein: 27 g; Carb: 18 g; Sugar: 2 g; Fiber: 3 g; Fat: 13 g; Sodium: 295 mg

SQUASH CASSEROLE   *Serves 6*

Some people look at the yellow squash in the farmers' market and wonder, "What should I do with it?" Here's an easy suggestion from me, and
I think you'll be very pleased with it.

2⅓ cups water

6 medium yellow squash, sliced
   into ½-inch pieces

½ cup chopped onion

I teaspoon Spike seasoning

½ teaspoon sea salt

I teaspoon flour

I tablespoon soy margarine

½ cup shredded Velveeta cheese

In large saucepan, bring 2 cups water to a boil and add squash and
onion. Boil for 10 minutes, remove from heat, and drain. Return to heat,
add ⅓ cup water, and continue to cook on low heat for 5 additional
minutes. Add seasonings and flour. Mix well. Add margarine and shredded cheese. Stir until cheese melts. Serve immediately.

Per serving: Calories: 103; Protein: 6 g; Carb: 12 g; Sugar: 5 g; Fiber: 4 g; Fat: 4 g;
Sodium: 375 mg

OVEN FRIED CHICKEN   *8 Servings*

Fried chicken is a wonderful American tradition, but old-fashioned methods of preparing this beloved dish just aren't healthy. I hope it will surprise you, pleasantly, that this oven-baked version is deliciously moist and full of flavor!

Vegetable oil spray

½ cup all-purpose flour

2 teaspoons Mrs. Dash seasoning

½ teaspoon sea salt

½ teaspoon black pepper

3½ pounds skinned, boneless chicken breast

Preheat oven to 425 degrees. Spray a 12" × 8" × 2" nonstick baking pan with vegetable spray until it is well coated and set aside. In a medium bowl, mix the flour, Mrs. Dash, salt and pepper. Set aside. Dip each piece of chicken into the flour mixture to coat well and place in the prepared baking pan. Bake chicken for 15 minutes, turn chicken over, and bake for an additional 15 minutes.

Per serving: Calories: 269; Protein: 45 g; Carb: 6 g; Sugar: 0 g; Fiber: 0 g; Fat: 7 g; Sodium: 240 mg

RED-HULL POTATO SALAD   *Serves 8*

Did you know that most of the nutrients in that grand vegetable, the potato, are in the skin or just underneath? That's the reason to prepare this
dish with the skins on. I also think that the potatoes taste better with
their rosy flesh intact.

6 medium red-skinned potatoes

1 small onion, chopped

3 tablespoons chopped dill pickle

½ teaspoon red pepper

½ teaspoon sea salt

⅔ cup low-fat Nayonnaise or
    low-fat natural mayonnaise

⅓ cup low-fat sour cream

Wash potatoes well and place in a large pot, cover with water, and bring
to a boil. Boil potatoes for 35 minutes or until fork tender but not falling
apart. Drain potatoes and allow to cool for 5 minutes. Place potatoes in
a large bowl. Use fork to break potatoes into large chunks. Add all other
ingredients and toss gently to combine completely. Cover and place into
refrigerator until cool.

Per serving: Calories: 164; Protein: 4 g; Carb: 25 g; Sugar: 4 g; Fiber: 3 g; Fat: 8 g;
Sodium: 364 mg

Delightful Desserts

Do desserts belong in a book about better nutrition? Some people may say no, but I am not one of them. I would never have been able to reach a healthy weight and stay there all these years if I had tried to eliminate desserts from my diet. Instead, I've accepted the idea that desserts are one of life's sweetest pleasures, and I've worked hard to create healthier versions of family favorites. That's not to say I eat cake every single day. I don't. I choose fresh fruit much more often. But for special occasions, for weekend dinners, and on days when I feel I deserve a healthy food "reward," these are some of the desserts I enjoy!

PINEAPPLE UPSIDE-DOWN CAKE   *Serves 16*

This is a beautiful, special-occasion cake, wonderful for birthdays, anniversaries, and the first day of spring . . . or just about any other time
you feel like celebrating!

1 stick (8 tablespoons) soy margarine	½ cup natural sugar
½ cup organic brown sugar	2 large eggs, preferably organic
1 (20-ounce) can crushed pineapple, drained	1 teaspoon vanilla extract
1 stick (8 tablespoons) soy margarine, softened	1½ cups all-purpose flour
	2 teaspoons baking powder
	½ cup soy milk

Preheat oven to 350 degrees. Melt 1 stick margarine in a 9-inch cast-iron
skillet over low heat. Add brown sugar and stir well. Turn heat off and
spread pineapple over the sugar mixture. Set aside. In a large bowl, use
a whisk to blend 1 stick margarine and natural sugar. With the mixer set
on medium speed, blend eggs into margarine mixture, one at a time.
Add vanilla extract and continue to beat. Combine flour and baking
powder. Beginning and ending with the flour mixture, gradually add
flour and milk and beat until batter is smooth. Pour prepared batter over
top of pineapple layer in skillet and bake for 30 minutes. Remove from
oven and place on a wire rack to cool. Carefully turn cake out onto a
platter, slice, and serve.

Per serving: Calories: 213; Protein: 5 g; Carb: 32 g; Sugar: 19 g; Fiber: 2 g; Fat: 7 g;
Sodium: 131 mg

JELLY CAKE SURPRISE   *Serves 16*

If your family loves jelly doughnuts but has given up those high-sugar, high-fat treats, give them back the pleasure *without* making them choose between good health and good taste.

1 tablespoon flour	1 teaspoon vanilla extract
1 stick (8 tablespoons) soy margarine, softened	1½ cups all-purpose flour
	2 teaspoons baking powder
½ cup natural sugar	½ cup soy milk
2 eggs	1 cup natural or organic jelly

Preheat oven to 350 degrees. Spray 9-inch cast-iron skillet with Pam or other cooking spray. Dust with flour and set aside. In a medium bowl, cream the soy margarine and natural sugar. With an electric mixer set to medium speed, blend the eggs one at a time into margarine mixture. Add vanilla extract and continue to beat until thoroughly blended. In a medium bowl, combine flour and baking powder. Add flour mixture and soy milk to batter, alternating, beginning and ending with flour. Pour prepared batter into skillet and bake for 30 minutes. Remove from oven and place on a wire rack to cool. Turn cake out onto cake plate. Using a piece of thread or sharp knife, gently cut cake horizontally. Spread half of the jelly on the bottom half of cake. Carefully set the top half on the bottom layer. Spread remaining jelly over top of cake.

Per serving: Calories: 175; Protein: 4 g; Carb: 31 g; Sugar: 19 g; Fiber: 1 g; Fat: 4 g; Sodium: 92 mg

SWEET POTATO CASSEROLE   *Serves 10*

Are you surprised to find this in the dessert section? In the Deep South, and in many other parts of the country, sweet potato pies and cakes are a beloved tradition. This casserole takes advantage of the natural sweetness of this tuber.

3 large or 6 medium sweet
   potatoes
½ cup organic brown sugar
⅓ cup pecans, chopped
½ cup sugar
2 eggs

⅓ cup soy margarine
½ cup soy milk
2 teaspoons vanilla extract
2 teaspoons flour
2 teaspoons soy margarine
   (to grease pan)

Preheat oven to 425 degrees. Scrub potatoes and prick deeply in several places so steam can escape. Place on a baking sheet and bake for 1 hour or until done. Remove from oven and allow to cool. Reduce oven to 350 degrees. When the potatoes are cool enough to handle, remove skin and mash potatoes in a large bowl. In a small bowl, mix brown sugar and pecans and set aside. In a medium bowl, combine sugar, eggs, margarine, milk, vanilla extract, and flour. Add mixture to sweet potatoes. Using an electric mixer at medium speed, beat the potatoes until creamy. Pour mixture into greased 12" × 8" × 2" baking dish. Sprinkle sugar and nut mixture over potatoes and bake for 30 minutes. Allow to cool before cutting and serving.

Per serving: Calories: 268; Protein: 5 g; Carb: 44 g; Sugar: 26 g; Fiber: 4 g; Fat: 8 g; Sodium: 68 mg

CHOCOLATE SILK CHEESECAKE   *Serves 18*

I didn't want to give up cheesecake, and so I put a lot of effort into coming up with a version I could enjoy while still keeping my heart healthy and my waistline trim. I'm so happy to share it with you!

I Graham Cracker Crust
   (page 156)
4 (8-ounce) packages Neufchâtel
   cheese, at room temperature
I cup natural sugar
½ cup soy margarine, melted
2 tablespoons cornstarch

2 tablespoons Hershey's Dutch
   Processed Cocoa
I teaspoon vanilla extract
2 teaspoons lemon extract
¼ cup unflavored soy milk
2 large eggs, preferably organic

Prepare crust and allow to cool.

Preheat oven to 375 degrees. In a medium bowl, using an electric mixer on medium speed, beat Neufchâtel cheese, sugar, and melted soy margarine. Add cornstarch, cocoa, vanilla extract, lemon extract, and soy milk and continue to beat until well blended. Add eggs, one at a time, beating after each addition until smooth and creamy.

Spoon mixture into prepared crust in springform pan. Bake for 35 to 40 minutes. Remove from oven and set pan on a wire rack to cool, about 40 minutes. Cover pan with plastic wrap, and put in the freezer for about 1 hour, or refrigerate for 3 hours.

Per serving, including the crust: Calories: 324; Protein: 9 g; Carb: 27 g; Sugar: 17 g; Fiber: 2 g; Fat: 20 g; Sodium: 317 mg

GRAHAM CRACKER CRUST

Yield: 1 (10-inch) crust

---

2 cups crushed graham cracker
   crumbs

2 tablespoons natural sugar

1 teaspoon unprocessed Dutch
   chocolate or carob powder

6 tablespoons soy margarine,
   melted

1 teaspoon ground cinnamon

⅓ cup pecans, crushed

Preheat oven to 325 degrees. In a medium bowl, combine all ingredients, mixing well. Firmly press crumb mixture evenly over bottom and sides of a 10-inch springform pan. Bake for 10 minutes and allow to cool before filling.

Per serving: Calories: 92; Protein: 2 g; Carb: 11 g; Sugar: 4 g; Fiber: 1 g; Fat: 5 g; Sodium: 79 mg

WATERGATE SALAD   *Serves 6*

This scrumptious pistachio and pineapple salad may have gotten its name from the scandal that led to President Nixon's resignation in 1973, but even after lots of Internet research, I can't find anyone who takes credit for naming it that! So the recipe name may be a mystery, but there's nothing mysterious about the popularity of this fruity delight!

I (20-ounce) can crushed
   pineapple, drained
I (4-ounce) sugar-free pistachio
   flavor instant pudding and pie
   filling

½ cup unsweetened coconut
½ cup pecans, chopped
1½ cups Cool Whip Lite

In a medium bowl, blend drained crushed pineapple and instant pudding and pie filling until well mixed. Stir in coconut and chopped pecans. Gently fold in Cool Whip Lite. Divide into six individual dessert dishes, chill for 30 minutes, and serve.

Per serving: Calories: 249; Protein: I g; Carb: 34 g; Sugar: 15 g; Fiber: 3 g; Fat: 12 g; Sodium: 795 mg

PECAN SANDIES   *Yield: 24 cookies*

Pecans are not only healthy but full of flavor, which is probably one of the reasons why so many cooks love to use them in desserts. These cookies are my own homemade version of an old-fashioned classic, and my students love them.

1½ cups all-purpose unbleached
   white flour

1 teaspoon baking soda

¼ teaspoon salt

¾ cup soy margarine or vegetable
   shortening

1 cup natural sugar

1 large egg, preferably organic

1 teaspoon vanilla extract

¾ cup finely chopped pecans

Preheat oven to 375 degrees. Combine flour, baking soda, and salt in a medium bowl; set aside. In another medium bowl, cream margarine and sugar using an electric mixer on medium speed. Add egg and vanilla extract and continue to mix. Gradually beat in flour mixture. Stir in nuts with a wooden spoon or rubber spatula. Lightly coat the inside of a small ice cream scoop (2 tablespoon size) with cooking spray, and use the scoop to drop dough on an ungreased baking sheet. Leave 2 inches between scoops of dough. Bake 12 to 15 minutes or until lightly browned. Allow to cool on rack for several minutes before removing from cookie sheet.

Per cookie: Calories: 138; Protein: 3 g; Carb: 18 g; Sugar: 9 g; Fiber: 1 g; Fat: 6 g; Sodium: 113 mg

BUTTER RUM SPICE DELIGHT CREAM   *Serves 10*

There are some very good nondairy "ice cream" products available, but since so many families enjoy using their ice cream makers, I wanted to offer this unique mixture that produces a very special dessert.

2 cups vanilla soy milk, rice milk, or
   skim milk, chilled
1 (12.3-ounce) box firm tofu,
   chilled
6 ounces Neufchâtel cheese

¾ cup natural sugar
1 teaspoon allspice
1 teaspoon vanilla extract
2 teaspoons rum extract

Place all ingredients in a blender or food processor. Process until smooth; pour into chilled ice cream maker container and freeze according to manufacturer's instructions.

Per serving: Calories: 148; Protein: 5 g; Carb: 19 g; Sugar: 17 g; Fiber: 0 g; Fat: 6 g; Sodium: 100 mg

BETTER THAN BLONDE

Yield: 24 pieces

Finding a way to make really good baked goods healthier is very important to me. Here's one that has been a favorite of all the kids who've tried it.

Vegetable oil spray

1 cup unbleached all-purpose white flour

⅓ cup oat or wheat flour

¼ teaspoon baking soda

1 tablespoon Dutch-processed cocoa powder

1 cup natural sugar

½ cup soy margarine

3 (1-ounce) squares white organic chocolate, melted

2 large eggs, preferably organic, beaten

1½ teaspoons vanilla extract

½ teaspoon lemon extract

⅛ cup water

⅓ cup pecans, optional

Preheat oven to 350 degrees. Lightly coat a 13" × 9" × 2" baking dish with cooking spray and set aside. In a medium bowl, sift together flours, baking soda, and cocoa powder; set aside. In another medium bowl, combine sugar, margarine, and melted chocolate. Use whisk to blend half the beaten eggs into the chocolate mixture. Whisk until almost creamy, and then add the remainder of the egg and whisk until mixture is creamy. Add extracts and water and continue to whisk until mixture is smooth. Gradually add sifted flour mixture. Using a large wooden spoon, stir in nuts, if desired. Spread mixture into prepared baking dish and bake for 18 to 20 minutes. Remove pan from oven and cool on rack. Allow brownies to cool in pan before cutting into squares.

Per serving: Calories: 117; Protein: 3 g; Carb: 18 g; Sugar: 11 g; Fiber: 1 g; Fat: 4 g; Sodium: 44 mg

For more of my healthier dessert options, pick up a copy of my *Dessert Lovers' Choice*.

Meeting Special Challenges 7

Eating Out,
Celebrations,
and Vacations

Once you've decided to commit to living sugar-free or at least drastically reducing your family's consumption of sugar, you still have to LIVE, right? So this is where you'll learn how to make this program work while facing all those everyday challenges every family has to meet: eating out just for fun or for special occasions; celebrating birthdays, anniversaries, or graduations; and vacationing, whether your destination is a family reunion or a favorite theme park.

Let me begin with one of the guiding principles of the *Healthy Kids, Smart Kids* program: it's up to you to decide what you put into your mouth, every single day. You have the opportunity with each meal, each mouthful, each nibble, to *choose* what you want to feel like, look like, and be.

But because we live *in* the world, because we share this planet with each other, we need to prepare ourselves, and our children, for living side by side with people who may not eat as we have chosen to do. What can we do to prepare ourselves for these occasions, and how can we develop confidence in meeting the challenges we all face?

In the previous chapters, you learned how to prepare your home and make healthy nutrition a comfortable part of everyday living. You "redecorated" your pantry and refrigerator, and you may have already begun to make changes in how, what, and when you feed your family. But beyond your front door is a world full of foods that can quickly reverse the positive effects of this program.

Here's the good news: you don't have to huddle together inside your home to maintain your new eating habits! But by planning, preparing, and understanding how to cope with the many temptations out there, you can keep your family focused on the goals you've chosen, and do it without feeling deprived and isolated.

> Browns Mill has taught me lots. Healthy food has changed my life because it helps my heart pump. It also helps me with my eyes. Healthy foods are also good for your taste buds to taste. The only reason I eat healthy foods is that they help my body. Being in a sugar-free school helps my mom and me a lot. When I go to certain restaurants, I always order healthy foods. That is why this school helps everyone in it.
>
> —*Rakim, third grade*

Eating in Restaurants, from Fast Food to Fine Dining

Most American families eat out at least three times a week, choosing drive-through fast-food meals on the way to soccer practice, opting for a Sunday supper at a family-friendly chain outlet, or celebrating a birthday or other special event in their town's best restaurant.

Here's the problem or, as I prefer to think of it, the challenge: the menus in all of these eating establishments are crowded with high-fat, high-sugar choices, from the traditional kids' meals composed of hamburger, french fries, and sugary soda to rich, buttery desserts at your favorite bakery cafe. How do you handle the temptations yourself, and how do you help your children to make good choices, when the whole world seems to be inviting you to "take just a taste"?

I believe that the best way to cope *and* save your sanity is twofold: plan ahead, and know what your options are. Arming yourself with even a little "edible education," you will find that meals at a restaurant can be delicious *and* healthful. You can eat meals that are good for you and for your kids by carefully choosing menu items, asking for smart substitutions, and explaining how you want your food prepared. When you remember that it's your money and your family's health at stake, you'll find the courage to speak up before you "pay up" for a meal outside your home or school.

Here are some good general guidelines for ordering a meal:

- Study the menu carefully to see what is available. You can even check out a restaurant menu online or call ahead. If you don't see what you want, ask if the kitchen can prepare something simple that your children will eat or that will adhere to your own special dietary needs.

- Be specific when you ask that a dish be prepared without a high-fat sauce or served with sauce on the side. If you feel embarrassed to be asking for special treatment, it can help to remind yourself that someone with allergies wouldn't hesitate to mention that to the server.

- It's possible, even likely, that even when you do your best to order healthy choices, some restaurant foods will contain "hidden" sugars and/or fats. Don't let that discourage you! Nobody's perfect, but making the effort really does make a difference when it comes to eating in a healthy manner.

• I'm a Southern woman through and through, but I've chosen loyalty to my health over a love for the deep-fat fryer! If I can do it, you can, too. Ask that your meats and vegetables be prepared baked, boiled, grilled, or steamed instead of fried. Fried food is high in calories as well as fat, so do your best to bypass that admittedly tasty "crunch." Your body will thank you! Another good reason to avoid fried foods: foods that are cooked in reused liquid fats at high temperatures just aren't heart healthy.

• When you're offered a choice of salad instead of fries, say, "Yes, please!" Even if the menu doesn't specifically provide healthier options, many restaurants will gladly serve you fruit instead of hash browns at breakfast, whole wheat bread instead of white, or a baked potato instead of onion rings, not to mention extra veggies on the side.

Meal by Meal—What Makes Good Sense When You're Eating Out
Breakfast

It's a fact: most fast-food breakfast items are very high in fat, while others are high in sugar, or both. Also, they're usually not very big servings, so you're inclined to eat more, more, more. If you're on a family road trip or eating breakfast out on a nonschool day, choose a diner or coffee shop if you can; they usually offer more and better healthy family options.

Fruit: Select any fresh fruit on the menu (berries, melon, bananas) or choose canned fruits packed in fruit juice or water instead of syrup. Your children may feel more satisfied if they order a piece of fruit instead of a small glass of juice.

Cereal: Hot or cold cereals such as oatmeal, Cream of Wheat, Raisin Bran, and shredded wheat are good choices. Add at least one-half cup of milk, and sweeten with sliced fruit or applesauce (delicious on hot cereal!). Check to make sure hot cereals are not prepared with cream or butter.

Eggs or protein: If you or your children opt for eggs, think about limiting egg yolks, which are high in cholesterol, to four to six per week. Ask for dishes made with egg substitute or egg whites. If you decide to order an omelet, your best bet is a veggie filling, and if you're concerned about weight gain, skip the cheese! Other good protein sources include lean Canadian bacon, lean turkey or chicken sausage, or soy protein products.

Bread: Whole-grain wheat or rye bread or toast is your best choice. A fresh bagel is an option, but bagels tend to be much higher in calories than the equivalent amount of bread. Ask for low-sugar fruit spreads, hummus, and low-fat or fat-free cream cheese instead of butter or regular cream cheese. French toast can be a reasonably healthy choice, but pouring buckets of syrup on top defeats the goal. Try fresh fruit or low-sugar jam instead. Avoid sweet rolls, doughnuts, muffins, and croissants. They contain unhealthy amounts of fat and/or sugar.

Beverage: Request low fat or fat-free milk for cereal. Drink coffee, tea, or decaffeinated coffee in moderate amounts and avoid powdered or liquid nondairy coffee creamers that contain unhealthy saturated fat.

Lunch

You've already read my recommendations for ideal brown-bag lunches in chapter 6, but sometimes you and your children will be eating lunch out. Again, consider your options and choose a restaurant that invites you to dine on healthy fare. Your best bet may be a salad bar or a shop like Subway, which offers made-to-order sand-

wiches prepared with lean poultry and meat, fresh veggies, and perhaps a slice of cheese.

Some other good ideas for mid-day munching include:

Soup: Some soups are high in sodium, but nowadays you're
likely to find the chef doing more with spices than dumping in extra
salt. Which soups offer your best bet for healthy eating? Creamy
soups are generally a no-no, though some menus list cream-style
soups that use low-fat dairy products and puréed vegetables, so ask.
Always good are bouillon, consommé, and broth-based vegetable
soups. If your family enjoys Mexican-style spicy cuisine, give gazpa-
cho a try, especially during the warmer months.

Sandwiches: Opt for chicken, turkey, tuna fish (individual can,
not tuna salad), or lean meat sandwiches. Grilled hamburgers made
with lean ground beef or turkey are good *occasional* choices. Be adventurous! Some restaurants offer vegetarian burgers or other meatless burger choices. Use reduced-fat mayonnaise, if you can get it. If
you can't, ask for mayo or dressing on the side and use it sparingly.
Skip most deli meats—bologna, salami, pastrami, or corned beef—
unless lean versions like those from Hebrew National or Healthy
Choice are available. I recommend avoiding sandwiches served with
gravy, as gravy is usually made with the fat drippings from the
cooked meat. (Mmm-mm, I know—good, but not good for you.)

Salad: Most restaurants offer lots of tasty luncheon salads, but
check out the ingredients before selecting one. Spinach, seafood,
grilled chicken, or fresh fruit salads are healthy options. If you order
a chef's salad, try to substitute lean poultry for one of the other
meats such as ham, roast beef, or salami. Don't succumb to the
"temptation of toppings." Skip items like crumbled hard-boiled egg
yolk, bacon, nuts, croutons, and most cheeses, or offer the kids a
choice of a couple, not all of them! Go for lots of fresh, raw vegeta-

bles, leafy greens, beans, and fresh fruit. Prepared salads like coleslaw, potato salad, and macaroni salad tend to be heavy with high-fat mayonnaise, so as the song says, "Walk on by." Opt for the lightest dressings possible, as many popular ones may contain several hundred calories in just one ladle, as well as a lot of unhealthy fat! Instead, use nonfat and reduced-fat dressings or vinegar, lemon juice, and other fat-free condiments to give your salads some zing! The best option is to ask for the dressing on the side so that you control how much you put on.

> The nutritional values here at Browns Mill have changed my life. Now I am very eager to get to lunch. It's like it's my favorite subject. After I'm finished eating, I feel recharged and ready to go. This food gives me energy to play and run around like I want to. This food has also changed my life because it keeps me alert in class, where I make straight As.
>
> —*Kendall, sixth grade*

Dinner

Just because you're eating in a restaurant doesn't mean that it's an occasion for putting healthy choices aside. If there's something special on the menu you decide is worth stretching the rules for, consider having it as an appetizer or sharing it with another family member. Some researchers have suggested that it's only the first bite or three that truly provide satisfaction, while the rest of a dish is consumed on automatic pilot! Also since restaurant servings are often oversized, you can always share or decide even before you are served to take part of your main dish home with you. The problem is that once that food is on the plate in front of you, it is sometimes hard to resist taking that next forkful . . . and the next, and the next.

If the waiter brings you a huge portion (two whole chicken breasts, three-quarter pound of roast meat), *don't eat it all*. It's clearly more than you can or should eat at a single meal. Ask to have it packed up so you won't be tempted to overdo. The good news is you'll have handy leftovers for packed lunches or fast suppers later in the week!

Let's talk about the ingredients that go into a healthy dinner out. First, should you order an appetizer? You may be surprised to hear that the answer is often yes. Order a glass of vegetable or fruit juice, a slice of melon, or perhaps a bowl of raw vegetables to start your meal. By satisfying your initial hunger with an appetizer, you won't feel so *ravenous* when the main dish is served. You're also much more likely to feel satisfied by eating a modest portion of your entrée.

A tossed salad made of leafy greens and other raw vegetables is always a good start to the meal. Sometimes children will enjoy fresh fruit salads with a side of yogurt. Ask for fat-free or low-fat salad dressing served on the side, or use salsa, vinegar, or lemon juice.

In many restaurants, bread is served automatically. Offer your children a slice, but suggest they try it without butter or margarine. In some places, olive oil is served as an alternative to butter, which is a much healthier choice, but oil is still high in calories and should be used sparingly. Your children may be surprised how good "the real thing" tastes! And my best piece of advice: don't ask for refills, even if they are offered!

Now let's discuss the main course. When I'm dining out, I will often select foods I rarely, if ever, prepare at home. Fresh fish dishes are great options, as are lean beef and pork in moderate portions. How can you tell what a portion is? Nutritional experts suggest that a three ounce serving of meat is the size of the palm of your hand or a deck of cards. It's not much, is it? That why I'm a fan of filling my plate with a variety of colorful, flavorful vegetables. I order my meat and fish broiled without added butter and/or salt, asking instead for a squeeze of lemon or lime juice or even a splash of wine. The alcohol will cook away, so only the flavor remains. I'll add steamed or grilled vegetables, plus some nutritious brown rice or potatoes (baked, broiled, or roasted) served *without* butter or high-fat sour cream. Try a baked sweet potato for a real treat if you can get it.

Finally, I recommend having dessert at home, after you've been digesting your food for a while. It's a great idea for several reasons: more choice about what you and your kids eat, a chance to save money on restaurant checks, and, ultimately, the opportunity to think about whether you're really hungry for it or are just eating dessert out of habit. If you do decide to have dessert at the restaurant, opt for fresh fruit, nonfat or low-fat frozen yogurt, sorbet, sherbet, sugar-free gelatin, or a low-fat cake such as angel food. But beware. Even low-fat choices may still have lots of sugar and be high in calories.

Eating Your Way around the World

Many families enjoy a culinary journey to another country when it comes time to eat meals outside the home. It's a great opportunity for children and adults to learn about another culture and maybe pick up a few words in a language other than English. Instead of your "usual" meal out of hamburgers or chicken, why not "eat exotic" instead? Here are some tips:

Chinese: Skip typical fried items such as egg rolls, wonton wrappers, fried rice, and fried noodles, and remember that "sweet and sour" is an extremely sugary sauce that should be avoided. Read menu descriptions with a detective's eye. Anything "crispy" is not a healthy choice. Your best bets are chicken, shrimp, and vegetable dishes that are steamed or stir-fried. If your children will try it, opt for something made with tofu, also known as bean curd, along with steamed rice. And brown rice is the nutritious one. Most Chinese dishes can be steamed and served with the sauce of your choice on the side.

Italian: This is a great choice for families because you can share large orders of pasta, and because pasta comes in many delightful shapes. Order your favorite pasta (penne, rotini, capellini) served with a fresh, light tomato sauce. Avoid cream-based sauces such as Alfredo and baked dishes that are topped with cheese (like baked ziti). Chicken, fish, and veal are good if they're prepared with nonoily sauces and are not fried or breaded. You'll be better off with a salad, for instance, than with melon wrapped in prosciutto. Select vegetable toppings rather than sausage or pepperoni on your pizza and skip the extra cheese.

Mexican: Many typical Mexican foods contain saturated fat, so ask about ingredients and choose carefully. Try to select chicken entrées such as fajitas and specify little or no oil in preparation. Skip the sour cream and use guacamole, made from avocado, sparingly. A chicken taco salad without the shell served with salsa is a good choice, as is a soft-shell chicken taco or tostada with little or no cheese. Ask for corn tortillas in place of lard-based flour tortillas. Salsa and hot sauces are fine, but definitely avoid refried beans that contain lard. Also, pass on any fried items such as chimichangas, flautas, and tortilla chips.

Steak House: Your best bet is to order broiled or baked fish, skinless chicken, Cornish game hen, or turkey without butter or gravy. If you do choose to have red meat, order a lean cut such as a filet mignon, flank steak, or London broil without butter. Avoid fried items. A baked potato, rice, and/or vegetables without added fat would be good side dishes.

Fast Foods

In 2004, a documentary film called *Supersize Me* made headlines when its creator reported health problems after eating nothing but fast food for a month! At the same time, as public concern over childhood and adult obesity rose and even a few lawsuits were filed by individuals blaming fast food for their weight problems, the major fast-food chains announced their response: McDonald's decided to stop offering its "supersize" option, and it also added a number of healthy options to its traditional menu. These included more salads, dressings that were lower in fat, bottled water, and even a handy pedometer for those customers who understood that exercise was part of a healthy living program. Many parents were pleased to see that Happy Meals could be customized for their children, allowing them to choose a side dish of apple slices instead of french fries, for instance, and offering the option of low-fat milk or bottled water instead of soda.

But even before these recent changes, fast-food restaurants had already begun offering alternatives to customers who loved the convenience of fast food but were concerned about meals that were high in fat and/or sugar. Kentucky Fried Chicken listed roasted chicken along with fried versions, and Wendy's small chili and grilled chicken sandwich were lower fat choices. And then there was Subway, with the inspiring story of its spokesperson Jared, who lost more than one hundred pounds while eating from their menu of healthy low-fat sandwiches! Unlike many fast food and chain restaurants, as Subway reminded consumers, it invited them to select only the items they wanted on their sandwiches, including an array of fresh veggies that would boost the healthy content of any meal.

Fast food as a family dining option isn't ideal, but it also isn't likely to go away. As our lives become busier and busier, many Americans are opting for fast food several times a week. But as long as people continue to request good nutrition along with speedy delivery, we're likely to see even more choices at our favorite drive-through!

Some general guidelines for ordering on the run are:

Sandwiches and wraps: Grilled chicken and turkey sandwiches and wraps are good; tuna that's made with light or nonfat mayonnaise is another good-for-you option. Ask for sandwiches made without added cheese, mayonnaise, and oil to decrease the saturated-fat content. Barbeque sauce (though this does have some sugar), mustard, vinegar, and ketchup (don't oversauce—this has sugar too!) are often the best condiment choices.

Noodle or rice bowls: Asian-style fast-food places offer many selections that are high in sugar and fat, but these bowls can "save" you. They're usually made with vegetables, chicken breast, white-meat turkey, tofu, or seafood. Brown rice is better than white rice, so order it if you can. Soy sauce is high in sodium, so order it on the side and use it sparingly.

Chicken: At restaurants like Boston Market or Kenny Rogers Roasters, choose rotisserie or grilled chicken over fried, and skip the skin. White meat is leaner than dark; better-for-you side dishes include baked sweet potatoes, oven-roasted potatoes, corn, squash, green beans, and salads of fresh greens. Avoid the coleslaw, potato salad, and other mayonnaise-rich salads.

Pizza: Choose thin crust over thick, and order vegetable toppings instead of pepperoni, ham, and sausage. Ordering a side salad delivers a more balanced meal than just devouring several slices.

Breakfast: A bagel with reduced-fat cream cheese may be your best bet, or a toasted English muffin with low-cal fruit spread if you can get it. Omelets made with egg whites or egg substitutes like Egg Beaters are also good. Limit the cheese to a light sprinkling on top.

Celebrations

I've had parents say to me, "Well, she can be sugar-free at school, but what about all those birthday parties she gets invited to?" Or, "We're going out to a special restaurant for Grandpa's eightieth birthday and I've ordered a whipped-cream cake. It would be just terrible if my son didn't partake of his granddaddy's birthday cake!"

I'll tell you what I tell them: taking good care of our health is a job we do every day of the year—365 chances to feel good and be at our best. Of course the world won't fall apart if your child has a piece of birthday cake on a special occasion, but your children need to get the message from you that making healthy choices is important.

This is especially true if your child is already overweight or suffering from early symptoms of serious medical problems like diabetes, high blood pressure, or even heart disease. No one would feel slighted if a diabetic passed on a piece of sugary dessert, would they? Of course they wouldn't. Or if a child with an allergy to nuts had to skip Aunt Mary's peanut butter cookies at a family picnic?

I'm reminded of a friend who kept this thought in mind when offered foods that she didn't want to eat because of health and diet concerns. "I'm sorry," she would say politely, "but I'm allergic." What she didn't add but always thought was, *I'll break out in fat!*

So many people today have health concerns, including many of our children, some who must avoid dairy products because of their asthma or who are allergic to this food or that. So it's not unreasonable to propose that you and your children *can* make healthy choices at parties, at dinners out—in fact, just about anywhere at all.

The fact is, if you've been avoiding sugar for a while, you may find that eating just a small piece of sweet dessert may leave you feeling a little sick or sluggish. Or maybe not.

A point I like to make when speaking to the children is this: a celebration is not about the food—or at least, mostly not about the food. It's about marking a special occasion with people you love.

Parties at School

At Browns Mill School, and throughout our county, we've taken what some people feel is a "shocking" step by selecting two occasions per school year on which we hold parties—*just two*. That means that we don't allow individual birthday parties in school, and that we don't have Halloween or Easter parties, either. Our two big events—and I do mean *big*—are a Winter Holidays Party and a Valentine's Day Party. Volunteer room representatives are responsible for planning the festivities for each classroom, and the children look forward to them with great excitement.

We send home a note at the beginning of each school year explaining the policy. It says, "As these are the **only** two county-level approved parties, **no other parties are permitted** during the instructional day. Parties that are held off school grounds, on weekends, or after school hours are not sponsored by the school and will not be supervised by school staff members. **Please do not bring or send balloons, cookies, cupcakes, birthday cakes, candy, ice cream, etc., to your child's classroom for any other occasions. If you would like some guidelines on the types of food items appropriate for the parties, please contact the homeroom teacher or the Front Office** [emphasis mine]."

Do you think the children in our school are being deprived of something important by missing out on all those cupcakes and liters of sugary sodas? I'm sure that many of our new students and parents may feel that way—*at first*. But once I explain that it's part of our commitment to the sugar-free environment and that we want our children to become used to alternative rewards and celebrations on these occasions, they "get" it.

Yes, some of the parents thought that if we did not have pounds of candy, sugarcoated cookies, and rich cakes for birthday parties, Valentine's Day parties, and winter holiday parties, the world would end. And the world as they knew it did end. But the children were much less concerned about missing out on those sweets. And they were happy with the new sugar-free world we'd helped to start.

When we asked our students to create a special healthy menu for our holiday parties and special events, they chose lemon-pepper wings, celery sticks with peanut butter and raisins, spiced popcorn, some of Dr. Butler's cookies (if she would bake them), trail mix, fruit bars, cheeses, and crackers.

They also told us that, more important to them than food, they wanted a party with some good music to dance to. Some of the kids stated that they would like their parents to spend the day with them on their birthdays or buy them a book or game that they could share with their classes instead of bringing a cake and ice cream. I shared their responses with our parents, who were very touched by the children's preference to spend time together as a family.

Our children have grown used to the idea that being fit is more fun than feeling sluggish, and that high test scores are better for polishing self-esteem than overstuffed bags of candy on Halloween. Our parents have joined us in our effort even outside the school, so that when neighborhood children go trick-or-treating at their homes, they receive *healthy snacks* instead of the usual chocolate candies.

There are so many wonderful products out there that will bring a smile to almost any child's face. I found organic gummy bears (Gummi Bears) at www.edwardandsons.com and St. Claire's Organic Tarts (just like Sweet Tarts, only made with natural colors and flavors) from www.shopnatural.com, just to name a couple of healthy goodies that are definitely kid approved. How about some Stretch Island fruit leather (100 percent natural ingredients and no added sugar—with flavors like Rare Raspberry, Mucho Mango, and Sweet Strawberry—from www.stretch-island.com)? Yum yum!

I mention these because even though we don't permit children's birthday parties in school, our children certainly celebrate with their friends at home—and there's no reason not to have a wonderful time while still enjoying good-for-you goodies. You'll find a selection of these in chapter 6, my "Recipes That Rock."

> Since I was four years old, anytime I would go to the store with my mom, I would always get a bundle of candy. Now I'm choosing my snacks right!
>
> When I first came to this school, I didn't like that Dr. Butler said, "Eat right, no sugar, because I love you!" Now I see that by making better food choices I feel better and my mind seems smarter. I love her.
>
> —Kedarien, third grade

Vacations

Once you leave the relatively safe confines of home and head off on vacation, you may feel that it will be difficult to maintain your healthy lifestyle on the road. But remember this: your concerns about foods high in sugar and fat are shared by families everywhere, and you've got lots of options to help you eat well just about anywhere you go!

The first question to consider is, How are you planning to get where you're going? If the answer is by airplane, your first assignment is clear.

High-Flying Foods

Consider this scenario: the kids are hungry, you're trapped at thirty-five thousand feet for anywhere from four to six hours, and the airline is offering a choice between cheesy lasagna and beef stew in gravy. This is assuming that they are offering anything at all! Do you just say, "Well, we'll eat whatever we're served."

You don't have to, once you practice planning a little ahead. Most of the major airlines are happy to provide, at no extra cost, meals that meet your dietary requirements. A recent check of the United Airlines Web site, for example, confirms that you can request diabetic, high-fiber, low-calorie, low-fat/low-cholesterol, low-protein, and low-sodium options, usually with just twenty-four to forty-eight hours' advance notice. Check with your airline to make certain. They often also offer a choice of a fruit plate, a kids' meal, and several different kinds of vegetarian meals.

Airline food still has its detractors, but you'll find that the special meals are frequently your best bet, and sometimes provide the added benefit of being served first, which can be great when you're traveling with children. A few years ago, asking for a low-fat meal meant you'd be stuck facing a dry chicken breast and a naked salad. Now you might be offered a tray featuring a whole grain roll with reduced-fat spread, a starter course of shrimp on a bed of lettuce with spicy cocktail sauce, tender roast chicken, vegetables that aren't at all soggy, probably some rice or pasta, and even a low-sugar oatmeal cookie for dessert!

All it takes to get a healthier meal in the air is a few extra moments when you're booking your flights. The alternative, if you are so inclined, is to prepare or purchase your own brown-bag meal so you decide exactly what you and your family are going to eat. It is also a good idea, especially for shorter flights when a meal is not served, to have a few healthy snacks, like trail mix, ready to give the kids. And always carry bottled water because you can get dehydrated quickly in an airplane.

On the Road Again

For many families, vacation travel starts in the car, so it's smart to be well prepared for the hours you're cooped up together on the way to your holiday destination. Travel with children is easier than it used to be, now that you can plug in a portable DVD player and entertain your kids for hours with their favorite movies.

But you've still got to think ahead when it comes to food, and most wise parents pack a cooler with exactly what they'll need on the road. Some of the best travel foods are those that come in their own perfect packages, like bananas, oranges, and hard-boiled eggs. It's a good idea to stick with foods that are easy on kids' stomachs: simple sandwiches on their favorite whole-grain bread, individual containers of applesauce and yogurt, and packages of low-fat crackers. Baggies of cereal also make good car snacks. To keep foods safe for serving, you will need a good cooler and ice packs.

If you can, plan to stop along the way so the kids can stretch their legs and get some fresh air. Maybe you can find a shady rest area or a park with picnic tables when it's time for lunch; you're likely to need a pit stop or two at some point along the way, especially if you give the kids some bottled water or juice during the ride.

Most children get restless during long car trips, so pack several small snacks to hand out at various intervals. Kids will enjoy the surprise and it will keep them from getting ravenous before you're ready to stop for a real meal. Good choices for travel snacks include

- Bags of baby carrots and celery sticks
- Fig bars

- Sugar-free puddings in individual containers
- Pretzels
- Granola bars

Skip those snacks that might cause choking (nuts, gummies), foods that are too messy (crumbly baked goods), or foods that may melt (ice pops, carob-covered energy bars). And don't forget to tuck in some disposable plates, napkins, and plastic tableware. You don't want to find yourself with a half dozen yogurts and no spoons! Also smart to include in your travel kit are a can opener, a good knife (Swiss army will do), and a large plastic bowl in case you open a bag of popcorn.

> Being sugar-free changed my life by making me pick healthy food groups. It gives me more energy.
> It's good to be sugar-free. I say that because it helps a lot. It's healthy. It's cool, too. That's what I think.
> —*Justin, third grade*

Stopping for Meals along the Way

If the only spot for a quick meal is a fast-food restaurant, you've got a list of good options in the eating-out section earlier in this chapter. If you've got young children and the place has a playground, allow some extra time if you can for the kids to get the kinks out after sitting for so long.

If you can find an old-fashioned diner, you'll have a few more healthy options: soup and a sandwich, an assortment of salads, even something from the entrée section like roasted chicken, a turkey burger, or a baked potato with broccoli on top.

Eating at Your Destination

When you're traveling as a family and planning a hotel or motel stay, it can be a great idea to book a room with a kitchenette. With a quick trip to the nearest market, you can stock it with healthy breakfast items, some juices, milk, and sandwich makings (tuna, turkey, peanut butter) if you want to go on an impromptu picnic. If your room comes with a microwave oven, a toaster, and a refrigerator, as well as cooking utensils and silverware, you'll be all set to save money on meals and to keep your kids and yourself well nourished.

Dining out with children can be a challenge even when close to home, so do check the menu of the restaurant where you're planning to have dinner to make sure it serves something your children will eat. If they're tired, they might just prefer getting takeout and watching a movie in the room.

Healthy eating on vacation is not only possible but possibly even easier than when you're at home. You've got a chance to open your kids' eyes to interesting regional foods and to point out items that are hard to get at home. Get ready to make some wonderful vacation memories together and to eat for good health every step of the way.

When I choose healthy foods, my brain gets smarter. When I go out, I choose healthy food choices like salad. Healthy food choices help your teeth. Sometimes when I go out, I choose healthy food choices so I won't get diabetes. When I go out, I might slip up and get a cheeseburger, but I will get right back on healthy foods.

Being at a sugar-free school makes it simple to choose, and the right foods keep me from getting fat. Choosing the right foods makes me a strong and smart person. When I eat too much sugar, I get fat stored in my stomach. That is why I choose sugar-free things. Browns Mill has shown me that my body is important.

—Nelson, third grade

Making Health and Fitness Part of the Fabric of Family Life

8

Shaping Your Child's Healthy Choices

We always talk about the parent being a child's first teacher, but it's not a cliché. We educators have the children for six or maybe a couple of more hours a day, five days a week. You have the children for all the rest of their waking hours, and during that time, your children are constantly observing you. The composer Stephen Sondheim, in *Into the Woods*, his musical based on fairy tales, warns that parents must be careful what they do and say because "Children Will Listen."

You've probably seen evidence of it, such as when a young child uses a word or expression in public that surprises or even shocks his or her parents, or, on the more positive side, when you overhear your children explaining to friends, using *your* words, why they will never smoke or use drugs.

Simply put, your children are shaped for better or worse by what you do. You are the primary influence in their lives, and because of that, the choices you make regarding health and fitness are likely to be the same ones that they make. If up to now you've been a fast-food junkie who never walked farther than from the front door to the car, you're not only slicing years off your own life, but you're probably cutting theirs short as well.

But no matter which unhealthy behavior choices you've modeled for your kids up to now, you can reduce and even reverse the damage by making the healthy changes called for in this book. By weaving these positive choices into your family's daily life, you will all see remarkable results over time in increased energy, more restful sleep, greater mental acuity, and, in most cases, a much lower risk of dangerous medical problems like diabetes, heart disease, high cholesterol, and high blood pressure.

You've already read plenty about how to get your family eating in a healthier way. You've learned to clean out your refrigerator, shop with pizzazz, and pack irresistible brown-bag lunches. Now I want to talk about another important ingredient in the "healthy living stew" I'm stirring up: boosting your family's heart rates and building fitness. Even if you currently consider yourselves members of the Couch Potato Club, you can begin a program of easy and fun activities that will not only contribute to better overall physical health but are likely to strengthen your family ties.

Remember those good old days before video games, computers, and big-screen TVs? Children couldn't wait to run outside and play after dinner and on weekends; kids just ran around for the pure fun of it! Now, though, staying active requires an "active" decision on your part, and a willingness to schedule activity into your busy life. Why? Because, as the old phrase goes, if you fail to plan, you plan to fail.

Fitting Fitness in

As an educator, I get plenty of pressure to squeeze all the important subjects into our school's daily schedule: reading, writing, math, social studies, science, and the arts, and somewhere in there, I have to make certain our students receive their mandated periods of physical education (PE). As a parent, you might feel that PE is an optional class, not especially important in this era of increased emphasis on standardized testing, but in fact, gym is a requirement in nearly every state in the United States. A recent study published by the Trust for America's Health noted that only two states—Oklahoma and South Dakota—do not require some form of physical education for their elementary school-aged students. And only six states—Alaska, Colorado, Kansas, New Mexico, Oklahoma, and South Dakota—do not require schools to provide health education.

But just because the state requirements exist doesn't mean that every school is providing those classes, nor does it mean that every student is getting what he or she needs. The laws are often not enforced, according to the same study, which was published as *F as in Fat: How Obesity Policies Are Failing America*. In a number of cases, the authors said, funds budgeted for these health and fitness programs are being diverted away to fulfill the federal mandates of No Child Left Behind.

The study is a real eye-opener because the programs vary so substantially from state to state. In Illinois, for instance, students are required to attend daily PE classes in grades K–12; in Arkansas, students are supposed to get one hour per week; and in California, the actual wording is "two hundred minutes every ten days" for elementary students.

In most cases, the duration and frequency of PE classes are not specified, just a vague requirement that students must receive PE. In Georgia, my own state, students are required to complete ninety hours of PE at each grade level in elementary school. Georgia students are required to receive ninety hours of health education each year as well, although many states are much less specific. These policies raise some serious questions: Are schools allowed to count recess time as part of fulfilling the PE mandate? Does a primary grade lesson on the parts of the body count as health education? It's unclear.

As obesity, diabetes, and a variety of heart-related illnesses among the country's young people inspire increased national concern, PE and health education in the schools are likely to get greater emphasis over the next decade. But the time to act is NOW. Do not wait until your town or city decides to put your children's health on the political agenda.

A Menu of Fitness Options

I turned to Browns Mill coach, Jeffrey Hughes, for assistance in bolstering the school's commitment to greater physical health for our students and staff. I believed then, as I do now, that a serious PE program, when partnered with a smart, sane nutrition program, is the best way to ensure that our children will grow up in the best of health.

As Mr. Hughes put it, "Both programs are striving to educate our students and faculty on the importance of exercising and healthy eating." With that as our goal, we began offering a weekly circuit-training course for our students throughout the school year. The course consists of stations where students jump rope, do push-ups or sit-ups, and perform step aerobics activities; we hope to add treadmills in the near future. We also offer step aerobics classes twice weekly and a walking club for our faculty and staff.

What's great about circuit training? It raises the heart rate, it requires a minimum of equipment, and it's appropriate for adults and children of all ages. Different activities keep exercisers from getting bored, and the different stations use a variety of muscle groups, which delivers the best kind of all-over workout.

Setting up a Circuit Course at Home

Before beginning this or any other physical fitness activity, please check with your family doctor. Your physician or other health professional can advise you what is safe and appropriate for you and your family to do.

It's easy to set up a circuit course in your backyard, if you've got one, or in a basement. Remember, you need to "warm up" before you start any fitness activity. An easy warm-up involves about five minutes of marching in place, arm swinging, and gentle stretching (no bouncing!). Then, once you begin the circuit, you also want to "warm down" between stations, usually by walking between them and taking some deep breaths. This is an aerobic activity, which means that the body needs to be getting oxygen while you're doing it! If you're out of breath, it becomes anaerobic and doesn't provide the same fitness benefits.

Here are some suggestions for stations that all members of the family can try.

1. Run in place for thirty to sixty seconds. Use a digital clock or just count to thirty or sixty.

2. Jump rope for thirty to sixty seconds. Alternate by jumping "pepper" with a single hop and doing the traditional jump that uses two hops.

3. Lie on a mat and do as many sit-ups as you can in one minute. Be sure to use the safest body position: knees bent and heels on the ground near your rear end. Your hands should be just touching behind your head. Be sure to use your abdominal muscles to do the sit-up rather than pulling yourself up with your arms.

4. On a mat, and on your hands and knees (or for more advanced exercisers, on hands and toes), do five to twelve push-ups. Make sure your body is aligned and back is straight.

5. Using a step platform and risers, if you have them, or a six- to ten-inch *stable* step stool, step up and down using the same leg for eight to twelve repeats, then switch legs. For more of a challenge, don't use the back leg to help you climb up, that is, no push-off.

6. For strength training, use two small dumbbells (three to five pounds) to do arm exercises:

- *Five to ten lateral raises*: With arms straight out to the side, raise the weights to shoulder level, then back to the starting position. Always exhale as you lift and keep wrists straight.
- *Ten biceps curls*: Hold the weights palms up, and start with arms hanging straight down close to the body. Lift the weights, bending from elbow to shoulder to ninety degrees, and return to start position.

If you don't have dumbbells, you can use filled plastic water bottles (a one-liter bottle filled with water weighs about two-and-a-half pounds). Just make sure the top is on tight!

7. Do twelve to twenty jumping jacks, depending on fitness level.

8. Do knee raises, lifting one leg at a time, bending the knee, and bringing it to hip height. Alternate, working quickly so your heart rate will increase.

Most circuit courses include from six to ten stations, so feel free to add your own and mix up the order in a way that works for your family. A circuit course is designed to be a cardio workout, boosting your heart rate and building endurance. But these exercises will also help develop strength and flexibility, which are important to overall fitness.

After completing the circuit course, it's time for a cooldown, which brings your heart rate down gradually and will help keep your muscles from tightening up after exertion. A cooldown can be quite similar to a warm-up, though it usually includes more gentle stretching and deep breathing.

Aim to use your circuit at least twice a week and three times if possible.

TOP TEN EXERCISES

The students at Browns Mill voted these ten exercises as their favorite ways to burn calories and build muscles, while having fun! Which of these will become your family favorites?

1. Walking	6. Aerobics
2. Jogging	7. Baseball/Softball
3. Dancing	8. Soccer
4. Jump rope	9. Skating (ice and roller)
5. Bowling	10. Swimming

Family Fitness Time

Finding the time to work out together or individually isn't easy, and there may be times when you just can't squeeze in a formal workout. That's a great reason to figure out lots of ways to "sneak" exercise into your busy schedule. It's easier than you might think, especially if you're creative, and if you remember that even ten minutes carved out of a busy morning and another ten minutes scraped out of a hectic afternoon, followed by another ten minutes or so after dinner, still delivers a lot of value when it comes to overall family fitness.

The simplest way to add some fitness minutes to your tote board is to walk instead of ride, or to allow extra time for a fast-paced stroll before you get where you're going. See if any of these might work for you and your kids:

• Instead of dashing for the bus at the last minute, plan to be ready ten minutes early and do a couple of lengths of your block before the bus arrives. Leave the backpack or book bag on the porch or front steps, though. The extra burden is too much for most kids to carry back and forth. If you've switched your child to a rolling cart, as many of our parents have decided to do, it's still better to walk or jog without it when your goal is exercise, not getting from point A to point B! And if you are looking for ways to make the time pass even faster, practice multiplication tables or addition facts as you walk along, or have your child teach you the words to his new favorite song. See if your daughter can name all the states or if your son can walk and spell at the same time!

• When you head out to go shopping, leave extra time to do a Tour de Mall (à la the Tour de France). Walk a speedy circuit of the level you enter on, then climb stairs to the next level and do the same. Cover all the levels and check out the newest stores as you stride down corridors, making sure to breathe. Speed walk past the food court, inhaling the tasty scents but not stopping to munch!

• Haven't ridden a bike in years but your kids love it? Pick up a used bike at a yard sale, get a helmet (required by law in many communities now), and share a pre- or postdinner bike ride through your neighborhood. You'll rapidly remember (or your body will) how to pedal, and the health benefits are as sweet as the extra time spent with your children.

• Dance! At Browns Mill we've had "dance marathons" for fund-raising events, combining good works with healthy activity, but you can incorporate this always fun fitness activity into your everyday life! Put on a CD or music channel while you're making dinner and encourage your children to dance along with you. It can be a great time to introduce different genres of music, from Tschaikovsky to jazz, Tejano to Broadway shows.

THE FAMILY THAT WALKS TOGETHER . . .

There's plenty of evidence that the buddy system works when it comes to exercise. If it's only up to you to get up and out when it comes to a workout, you're more likely to turn over and go back to sleep or to change the TV channel and settle in on the sofa. But if you've got a fitness "date" with a friend or a family member, studies have demonstrated that, at least most of the time, you'll show up.

Why? There are many reasons. We're social animals and prefer being together to being alone. We're subject to feelings of guilt and hate to let anyone down. Or maybe we just can't think of a really good excuse not to go—one that the other person will accept!

Whatever the reason, exercising together is a healthy habit, which is a great reason to organize a family fitness team to work out at the same time. It doesn't have to be a formal exercise session every time. Just making a date to go for a postdinner walk around the neighborhood or a group bike ride on a weekend morning will quickly pay off, not only in better health for all but also in real feelings of togetherness as a family.

The latest fitness recommendations suggest that everyone aim to move ten thousand steps a day, so why not invest in pedometers for all and chart your progress on a poster in the kitchen or den? A regular schedule of family fitness walks provides a terrific opportunity to talk as a group or one-on-one with different members of the family.

By working to get fit together, even the busiest family will strengthen the emotional ties that sustain them. Instead of sprawling on sofas watching a movie and saying nothing to each other, get up, get out, and get reacquainted!

Setting Special Goals

Sometimes what makes the difference in a child's enthusiasm for an activity is the sense of purpose that accompanies it. I've seen a remarkable transformation in children whose initial interest in exercising was minimal but who changed their tune when they were encouraged to train for a charity event.

Our students and faculty have participated in a number of these fund-raisers, and their efforts have generated more than money for a series of good causes. In many cases, students began by learning about a particular ailment or medical concern in a health class or science lesson. Once armed with the facts, they developed a vested interest in helping to fight the disease by finding a cure, so their motivation to do what it took soared sky-high!

One fund-raiser that has become an annual event for our Browns Mill family is the American Heart Association's Jump Rope for Heart. All proceeds go toward research and to help people with various cardiac concerns. The kids learn to jump rope and build endurance in their PE classes, so it's natural for us to join in this particular effort. It also ties in beautifully to what the students have been learning in their study of healthy habits and good nutrition. In a recent year, our students and faculty jumped for hours (not all at once, but at different times at the jumping activities our coaches scheduled over the course of a week) and raised nearly $3,000! But just as important, our efforts on behalf of others contributed to our own improved health and fitness.

We've also done walks to raise awareness for diabetes and to help raise funds to fight breast cancer, among others. All of these illnesses have touched people that the children know in their community, which makes the fund-raising and the physical training required to do the event *personal.* I think that's the key: helping the students understand that they are part of a greater world, and their contributions can truly make a difference in people's lives!

Why not organize your family into a team for an upcoming charity event in your community? There are so many choices, depending on where you live. In New York, children and adults raise money for multiple sclerosis research by riding their bikes all around the city, while in California, school kids run laps around a field and get sponsors to support their efforts. Elsewhere, students put on dance marathons, swim relays, and roller skate for a plethora of good causes. It's a great way to teach children about community service while having a good time together!

Other benefits of raising funds for charity through fitness include the following:

- Kids practice real-life math skills by calculating how much money they can raise when donors pledge a certain amount per lap.
- Children develop communication and presentation skills when requesting contributions from family and friends.
- Students build self-esteem and pride by setting challenging goals and working hard to reach them.

There's a wonderful phenomenon that comes with exercise, something that used to be referred to as "the runner's high." Well, you don't have to be a runner to experience the burst of endorphins that are released by your body when you work out and break a good sweat. It happens when your muscles are stressed in a good way and release a substance into your bloodstream that actually mimics the effects of some feel-good drugs. They are actually "polypeptides," a combo of thirty amino acids that help to block pain signals produced by the nervous system.

Research has demonstrated that this rush of good feelings can boost athletic performance, get you through momentary discomfort

---

STARTING THE DAY

At Browns Mill School, we made a commitment to help our children and staff members live their best possible lives. To start every day in the healthiest possible way, the entire school stretches every morning—in their classrooms and offices—to release stress and tension before the day begins in earnest. We have a wonderful meditation tape that we play over the intercom, led by Tanjala Wright, an inspiring woman who helps us set the tone for a good day—every day!

---

and aching muscles, give you that sensation known as the "second wind," and get you to the finish line or the end of your workout in great spirits!

Endorphins also appear to reduce overall stress, provide anti-aging benefits, and even strengthen the immune system. Do you need any better reasons for fitting regular exercise into the fabric of your family life? I certainly don't; I'm convinced!

Some research suggests that eating chocolate also produces an endorphin release, but the high sugar content in most chocolate can have other negative effects on your body. Instead, you and your kids can experience the intense, pleasurable, positive feelings you used to get from gobbling down high-sugar snacks by exercising your bodies instead of your sweet tooth. Then you can celebrate your workout's end with a delicious smoothie or piece of ripe fruit, and get double the health benefits.

Being sugar-free changed my life. I exercise more, I read the labels on food items, and I do everything I can to stay healthy.

I *never* will or plan to eat a lot of candy at home just because I'm out of school. I will stay sugar-free for the rest of my life!

—Jasmine, third grade

Growing the Dream  9

How to Help
Bring about Change in
Your Local Schools

The French writer Victor Hugo wrote, "There is one thing stronger than all the armies in the world, and that is the power of an idea whose time has come!" Everywhere I've spoken to groups, and after every media appearance, the response to this program from people across the United States persuades me that parents everywhere are ready to create a health revolution in our public schools.

They've listened to the frightening statistics about the obesity epidemic among our children, they've heard the disturbing predictions that this could be a generation of young people who may not outlive their parents, and they've understood—because the problem is so close to home—that if change is to be, as the quotation goes, "it's up to me."

I'm happy to report that you are part of a rising tide of public opinion, that your call for action is echoing in cities and towns all over the country, and that almost every day there is new evidence that a seismic change has begun to take effect. In school districts from California and Wisconsin to New York and points south, change is under way, and it's just in time.

The Evidence That Demands a Shift in
What We've Always Done

In May 2004, the *New York Times* reported new guidelines for pediatricians that advised them to treat high blood pressure in children as "aggressively" as they do in adults. In the past, doctors had believed that another illness, such as kidney disease, was responsible for hypertension in children, but new evidence suggested that it was similar to what adults suffer and put affected children at risk for elevated cholesterol and early diabetes, as well as organ damage such as enlargement of the heart.

The article went on to note that while weight loss and exercise were advised initially, the report told doctors to consider prescribing blood pressure medication to children who didn't respond quickly enough to other treatment.

A month later, Dr. Ileana Vargus, a pediatric endocrinologist at New York Presbyterian Hospital Naomi Berrie Diabetes Center, reported that type 2 diabetes, previously an adult disease, was turning up in disturbing numbers in New York City children. "It's happening nationwide, but it's happening more in urban areas like New York." She added, "It's happening a lot more in African-American and Hispanic children, but Caucasian children are by no means immune, because the risks have been steadily increasing across the board since the 1970s."

The American Diabetes Association concurred, noting that in the past, most children developed type 1, or juvenile diabetes, but that now, up to 45 percent of new diagnoses were type 2.

In type 2 diabetes, "less and less sugar is cleared from the blood and stored in cells," said Cathy Nonas, director of diabetes and obesity programs at North General Hospital in Manhattan (in an interview in the New York *Daily News*). With a type 2 diagnosis comes fear of increased risk of cardiovascular and kidney disease as well as nerve damage and even blindness. The article went on to note that as many as 45 percent of New York City schoolchildren met the clinical definition of obesity, and further quoted doctors suggesting that what children eat during the first years of life plays an important role in how their bodies develop. When kids eat mostly simple sugars and refined sweets, high-fat and calorie-dense fast foods, and highly sweetened cereals, these potential "villains" cause the risk of type 2 diabetes and subsequent complications to rise precipitously.

By October 2004, the Institute of Medicine, part of the National Academy of Sciences, a private, nonprofit organization that advises the federal government on science and health policy issues, issued a no-holds-barred report that recommended extensive changes in American society to keep our children healthy. In the following list based on reports in the *Atlanta Journal-Constitution*, the panel suggested a number of immediate actions be taken:

• The federal government should develop nutrition standards for foods and beverages sold in schools, fund nutrition and physical-activity grants for states, develop guidelines for marketing to children, and expand research.

• The food industry and media should develop healthier food and beverage products, provide better consumer nutrition information, and provide clear and consistent messages about food and health in the media.

• State and local governments should increase opportunities for physical activity in communities and work to expand access to healthy foods.

• State and local education authorities and schools should improve the nutritional quality of foods served and sold in schools, increase opportunities for more physical activity during and after school, create programs to reduce the number of hours children spend watching TV and playing video games, and develop wellness programs for their communities.

- Health-care professionals should start recording body mass index information on their patients and track changes, providing assistance to families and children.
- Community and nonprofit organizations should offer high-risk populations more access to healthy eating and physical activity as part of their programs.
- Parents and families should reduce sedentary behavior and actively pursue more healthful eating and physical activity.

Whew! The solutions proposed are wide ranging and potentially costly, but the dangers are equally serious. Obesity-related disease costs more than $129 billion annually in this country, according to one estimate, and that doesn't include the emotional and psychological costs for children growing up overweight and unfit.

Currently there are a number of programs around the country working to curb childhood obesity, but as a survey commissioned by Shaping America's Youth discovered, these initiatives aren't reaching enough children, nor are they focusing on strategies that are considered most likely to work.

Dr. David McCarron, the organization's executive director, discussed the results of a recent study (whose respondents included eleven hundred organizations that work with children), noting, "If you look at the data, most of the programs are directed at the middle school years and older, yet we know that if a child enters first grade and is overweight, he or she is [more likely] to be overweight" for life.

His concerns were echoed by Dr. Carden Johnston, president of the American Academy of Pediatrics. "Adult diseases begin in childhood, so once you become an obese adolescent, you become an obese adult and that becomes a life-shortening disease."

What's not working in these programs studied? More than three-quarters of them ran for less than a year, only 8 percent involved the entire family, and in many cases, the program contacted the children once a week or even less. Furthermore, the programs focused on providing students with information instead of actually helping to alter the children's daily environment in ways that contribute to reaching and maintaining a healthy weight.

Dr. McCarron, whose organization includes as members the office of the Surgeon General, the American Academy of Pediatrics, and Nike, added, "Our hope is in prevention. That's why we need to direct our efforts to infants, toddlers, and preschoolers because that's where it needs to start." He went on, "Parents need to understand, in the early stages of a child's life, they need to be setting a

> The nutrition program at Browns Mill School has affected my life by helping me become aware of what I eat. The nutrition program helped me sportswise because it has helped me become long winded. Long winded means to be able to run longer.
>
> It has also helped me by the water vending machines. The water vending machines have made a lot of money by the kids in the school purchasing the water bottles.
>
> The news crew is always up here interviewing some of the kids about the nutrition program. It is one of the most unique programs in the state. I think that all schools should try the nutrition program.
>
> —Jordan, sixth grade

pattern of exercise and eating that is conducive to maintaining a healthy weight."

That's it. *There's* your mandate. Now, what can you do to make this happen in your community?

What Are Other Parents Doing?

In the July-August 2004 issue of *Children's Advocate*, published by Action Alliance for Children, I learned about a Los Angeles parent named Arely Herrera, who joined a campaign to fight for healthier school food for her children. As part of the Healthy School Food Coalition (HSFC), she helped win an important victory. Because of her work and that of many other concerned individuals, Los Angeles Unified School District (LAUSD) students will now be offered healthier snacks and salad bars, among other changes described in the district's Obesity Prevention Motion.

A grassroots group of parents, teachers, administrators, and students, HSFC was formed with the help of Occidental College's Center for Food and Justice. The center had previously worked with selected schools but realized they couldn't make districtwide changes without a major campaign.

Campaign Director Francesca De La Rosa gives the credit for the campaign's success to "parents—prepared and aggressive—from low-income neighborhoods, primarily Spanish speaking." Participants took workshops on nutrition, which served as a personal call to arms. Herrera said that the nutrition training "helped me help my husband take care of his cholesterol." She started serving healthy recipes and adds that now her kids eat vegetables "without complaining, because they don't notice they're eating cauliflower."

How did the HSFC team make it happen? They spoke with other parents who were waiting to pick up their kids, made presentations at school PTA events and school board meetings, spoke privately to administrators, got signatures on petitions, and even sent gifts to members of the school board—jars of sugar, vitamin bottles, and organic fruit baskets—before the issue came to a vote.

When some insisted that cafeteria food was fine just as it was, HSFC members arranged to provide samples of what their children were being served. When others expressed doubt that students would accept more fruits and vegetables instead of the usual fare, HSFC made its case by offering bowls of fruit in cafeterias, then watching as students eagerly devoured them.

As in many school districts, concern was expressed about income earned from soda sales as opposed to what they might earn when those machines were replaced with water and juices. But ultimately, the health of the Los Angeles students took precedence, and the HSFC won its case.

Starting Young

At the same time the HSFC was taking on the LAUSD, a Children's Aid Society program called Go!Kids was doing its part to teach families how to live and eat for better health. While a nutrition consultant prepared a soy-based salad dressing and explained the difference between healthy and unhealthy fats to a group of twenty Head Start mothers in one room (with Spanish translation provided), a classroom of preschoolers at PS 5 in Washington Heights was singing. "We need food that makes us go," they shouted. "Greasy food only makes us slow."

These parent and child classes are part of a new initiative designed by the Children's Aid Society, a 150-year-old nonprofit social service agency, to prevent childhood obesity. Helping preschool-aged children develop healthy nutrition habits and make physical activity a part of their everyday routine is the latest mission the society has chosen to focus on.

But in Washington Heights, many factors make it harder for this largely Dominican community to incorporate the healthy eating behaviors they're learning. Dr. Paula Elbirt, a pediatrician and the medical director of the Children's Aid Society, noted that many parents feel the playgrounds and parks aren't safe, so they don't take their children there to play. There is also a "perception that exercise is for rich white people," she added, "and you have to spend a lot of money" to get it regularly. The local markets don't sell a lot of fresh fruits and vegetables because they're not in demand, so Dr. Elbirt has been urging the mothers to request more fruits such as mangos, which, like potatoes and yams, are mainstays of dishes served in Dominican households. The message that Go!Kids and the Children's Aid Society are trying to send is one of balance and moderation: a reminder that parents and children can and should work together to make healthy choices.

Concern about poorer families' access to a variety of fruits and vegetables to serve their children was cited in a study published in late spring 2004 in the *American Journal of Public Health*. In a Reuters Health interview, the study's author, Dr. Mary Ann Chiasson, explained that while many people may associate poverty with not having enough food, poverty usually means eating only inexpensive foods, which are often unhealthy. Fresh fruits and vegetables are very expensive, she noted. "I think it is much harder to eat healthier foods when you're low-income."

During the study, Chiasson and her team asked 1,255 families whose children were enrolled in the New York City Special Supplemental Nutrition Program for Women, Infants, and Children (WIC), a branch of the federal nutrition program for poor families, to complete a questionnaire about family diet, background, and exercise habits. They also calculated 557 children's body mass index (BMI), which factors height into a person's weight.

Researchers found that 22 percent of the children were overweight, meaning they had BMIs in or above the ninety-fifth percentile for their gender and age. Another 18 percent had BMIs that fell between the eighty-fifth and ninety-fifth percentile, indicating

---

WHAT DOES A TYPICAL SCHOOL LUNCH LOOK LIKE?

From Alaska to Texas, from Iowa to South Carolina, public school districts feed millions of American children at least one meal a day, sometimes two or more. What's on the menu in a typical school lunch? Here's a "snapshot" of what I found early in 2005:

Anchorage, Alaska

Pizza or fried burrito, vegetables with dip, sliced pears, milk

Charleston County, South Carolina

Low-fat Corn Dog with Ketchup and Mustard, Steamed Broccoli and Cauliflower, Minute Maid 100 percent Fruit Juice Bar, Royal Brownie, Milk

Des Moines, Iowa

Honey BBQ Pork Rib Patty on a Bun or Char-Grill Chicken Patty on a Bun, Oven French Fries, Celery and Tomatoes with Dip, Orange Wedges, Oatmeal Cookie

Abilene, Texas

Spaghetti Casserole, Chicken Nuggets with Gravy, Baked Potato with Butter, Broccoli with Cheese Sauce, Pudding with Topping, Hot Roll, Choice of Milk

Exeter, New Hampshire

Lasagna or turkey salad sub, roll, green beans, fruit, pudding

What can this quick look tell us about how American students are eating? Some schools appear to be offering more healthy choices, including more vegetables; others may need to review the latest recommendations on lowering fat in children's diets.

they were at risk of becoming overweight. Only 5 percent of children were underweight, meaning their BMIs fell below the fifth percentile. They also discovered that Latino children were more than twice as likely to be overweight as other children, and that three- and four-year-olds were 36 percent more likely than two-year-olds to be overweight or at risk of developing a weight problem.

In the nutrition surveys, they also learned that 73 percent of the children drank whole milk, and about 44 percent ate fruits or vegetables less than once each day. Making a strong case for early intervention, Dr. Chiasson said, "Waiting until these children start school may be too late."

How Some Parents Are Getting Involved

Sara Tedeschi had decided to volunteer at Shorewood Hills Elementary in Madison, Wisconsin, to help ease her children's transition from a rural community to this big-city school, but helping to supervise the students' lunch period once a week was a disturbing eye-opener.

The students were served strange-looking food in vacuum-sealed pouches; nothing was fresh and most lacked significant nutritional value. Most kids raced through the meal so they could play outside, leaving a mountain of wasted food.

I read about Tedeschi's experience on the Connect with Kids Web site, and I was inspired by the efforts she is making to bring better food to the children in her community.

"I thought about the daily message that lunch sends, what kids learn from doing this day in, day out," she explained in an interview by Douglas J. Buege. An organic farmer and nutritionist, Tedeschi expressed concern about a society where our children get mixed messages, where anorexia exists alongside epidemic obesity. Calling the kids' experience at lunch a "hidden curriculum" about food and eating, Tedeschi believed that what they learned in the lunchroom would likely contribute to health problems later in life.

What were these negative "lessons"? A view of food as a factory-processed product completely unrelated to its original form. "It's all pretty far from the farm, the fields, the soil, sun and water," she noted. She also felt the students were unaffected by the piles of wasted food and the cost, not only in dollars but in terms of the environment.

Beginning in 2002, Tedeschi began working with an organization called REAP (Research, Education, Action, and Policy) food group, a group of farmers, restaurateurs, nutritionists, professors, students, and other concerned citizens who were already working to bring healthy meals to college cafeterias. She found that there were programs in place around the country to help children make the connection between the food they consumed and the people who grew and harvested it. Alice Waters's Edible Schoolyard Project in Berkeley, California, was a model for what she hoped to accomplish. The one-acre garden Waters helped create boosted the science program at Martin Luther King Middle School, where students learn about food by growing, harvesting, and preparing it themselves. And in Santa Monica, California, all fifteen of the district's schools offer a daily salad bar stocked with locally grown produce.

Tedeschi worked with REAP to form Wisconsin Homegrown Lunch, a program with three ultimate goals: providing healthy produce to kids eating school lunches, creating a reliable and profitable market for local farmers, and educating the public. The program started with three elementary schools in the fall of 2002 and invited farmers to provide classroom tomato and apple tastings, give Farmer in the School presentations to the children, and host field trips to their farms so students could understand where the food came from.

Wisconsin Homegrown Lunch staffers generated support by connecting with parents through sending out regular newsletters and by appearing at PTA meetings and school social gatherings. They made a special effort to reach out to Madison's large Hmong (from Laos) and Hispanic communities. They held potlucks, served organic produce, and spread the word.

Tedeschi admits that it's been easier to build support than to get healthy foods into the schools, but says they will continue to work toward that goal. One of the difficulties she cites is the price point of the school lunch. At the time this article appeared, it was $1.70, which made it hard to put organic food on the menu. One option being considered is a centralized kitchen facility to process foods into more ready-to-use packaging that would save money. In the meantime, school lunches do include plenty of baby carrots, broccoli florets, and iceberg lettuce. Tedeschi is also hoping that local products—cranberries, maple syrup, and dairy items—will be added to school menus. In the meantime, Wisconsin Homegrown Lunch has helped develop new meal items that have been tested in the schools. Some student favorites are veggie wraps, squash bisque, and egg rolls.

For parents hoping to do something similar in their communities, Buege's article mentioned government programs like the USDA's Sustainable Agriculture Research and Education (SARE) program, which provides support for farm-to-school initiatives. In 2003 there was a bill pending in the U.S. House of Representatives (the Farm-to-Cafeteria Projects Act, part of HR 2626, its Child Nutrition Bill) and a corresponding bill in the Senate (S 1755) that would provide $10 million annually in $100,000 lumps for school districts or non-profit organizations establishing farm-to-school projects. (As this book goes to press, HR 2626 had been referred to the Subcommittee on Education Reform. It has not yet been reintroduced.)

The Farm to School Program

The Farm to School Program is a leader in the effort to incorporate healthy and nutritious produce into school lunches, snacks, and salad bars. As the organization states on its Web site, "Anyone who has picked a tomato right off the vine knows that a great tasting tomato is synonymous with freshness. We want kids to know that fresh produce tastes great!"

The major goals of the Farm to School Program are to partner local farmers with nearby schools so that (1) children can enjoy tasty fruits and vegetables while connecting with farms, the source of their food; and (2) farmers can develop an additional source of income.

Some Farm to School projects follow:

- At the Farmers' Market Salad Bar in Santa Monica, California (mentioned above), the produce is purchased at the farmers' market twice weekly to provide for a daily salad bar with California-grown produce. (Organized by the Occidental Community Food Security Project.)
- In North Carolina, the state legislature gave grants to schools to purchase farm products. This initial jump start led to continuing purchases of farm produce, with the state department of agriculture providing transportation, warehouses, and administrative services. (Organized by the USDA and the North Carolina Department of Agriculture.)
- The New North Florida Cooperative was formed by local small farm operators to sell produce to schools. As well as strawberries

and melons, they provide turnip and collard greens that are fresh, washed, chopped, and bagged to the local school district. (Organized by farmers.)

Interested in bringing Farm to School to your county? For more information, contact

Marion Kalb
Farm to School Program Director
Phone: 530-756-8518, ext. 32
Fax: 310-822-1440
E-mail: marion@foodsecurity.org

Assistance will be provided on a variety of topics, including how to find farmers, working with school food service directors, and creating a town hall meeting.

Also provided by Farm to School, some possible funding sources for Farm to School Programs are listed below:

www.csrees.usda.gov
Community Food Projects Competitive Grants Program, Fund for Rural America, Community Food Projects, Community Supported Agriculture, and a variety of other funding programs are listed here. A must-see.

www.rurdev.ocd.usda.gov
Looking for notices of funding availability, search by department, grant deadline, and key words.

www.fns.usda.gov/fns/
Site lists grants for state agencies, including Team Nutrition and Federal State Marketing Improvement Program (FSMIP).

www.communityfoundationlocator.com
Site lists foundations by state with an easy-to-use U.S. map graphic. It also uses maps to show locations of each community foundation.

www.granted.org
Corporate and community foundations are listed by state or grant category with links on grant writing. Grant categories include environmental, nonprofit organizations, and agricultural farming resources.

www.rurdev.usda.gov
Listing Rural Business Enterprise Grants and Rural Business Opportunity Grants, this site focuses on funding for agricultural marketing and production innovations.

www.sare.org
Organized by region, the creators of this site fund new markets for farmers. They also fund multi-institutional, collaborative approaches including nonprofit organizations, university staff, and farmers.

In some states, the state health department may have funding available through the Nutrition Network. The following states have Nutrition Network programs:

Alabama	Iowa	New Jersey	Virginia
Arizona	Kansas	North Carolina	Washington
California	Maine	Oklahoma	Wisconsin
Colorado	Michigan	Pennsylvania	
Georgia	Missouri	South Dakota	
Indiana	Nevada	Vermont	

A Private-School–Public-School Partnership

Ann Cooper, executive chef and director of Wellness and Nutrition at the Ross School in East Hampton, New York, serves regional, organic, and sustainable foods for both breakfast and lunch. Nutritious, locally grown products have replaced junk food, just as sitting down at a table, after checking one's shoes, has replaced eating on the run. This private school has extended its program to include serving Ross food at the Bridgehampton public school, and a Kellogg grant has made it possible for Cooper to extend the program to New York City public schools.

Cooper says, "Educating kids is part of a bigger wellness program—tied to exercise and health. The cafeteria is considered a classroom. If a child says that they do not like math or reading, we don't say, 'Fine, you don't have to learn that.' The same ideology must be seen in regards to nutrition. If a child says they do not like a certain food, they need to be educated about their food choices, not just acquiesced to poor nutrition choices, and often just because it's easier."

The school's students have to learn to cook to graduate at Ross, where they daily bake breads and pizzas, make soups, offer a complete salad bar, and offer at least one vegetarian entrée each day; they serve almost no processed foods, refined sugars, refined flours, soda, candy, or junk food.

Cooper adds, "We emphasize the role of local farmers and their farms, from which the majority of our food comes. We teach the importance of eating organically, explaining why our health and the earth's future depend on it."

DR. BUTLER'S KEYS TO PROMOTING HEALTHY EATING IN SCHOOLS

• You can't do it alone. For a program that will truly transform your school, students, parents, and teachers need to be involved in developing a shared vision for a healthy eating environment.

• Once a vision for the program has been developed, the team needs to decide how the total school environment can support the development of healthy eating patterns. For us, this meant removing soda machines from the cafeteria and enlisting the support of vendors nearby.

• Knowledge is power! Provide nutrition education to all staff members from support staff, like custodians, aides, and community volunteers, to teachers and administration.

• Work those menus! School meals must meet USDA nutrition standards, but there are many ways to do that. Explore your options and choose what is healthiest *and* doable.

• Highlight success so those "on the fence" will hop on the bandwagon! Students, teachers, and parents who practice healthy eating habits will be encouraged to act as role models in the school dining areas; peer mentoring works!

• If you can't ban 'em, beat 'em! Work with suppliers so that snacks provided in school vending machines are the healthiest you can get. As more healthy products are offered in snack-size packages, you'll have plenty to choose from.

Change Begins at Home—and in Your Hometown

Now that you've read about what other parents and communities are doing to address the challenge of improving the foods in their schools, it's your turn. Here are some suggestions to help you get started:

• Get the facts. Collect school menus, visit the cafeteria if possible, and talk to your children about what eating in school is like.

• Reach out to other parents and concerned members of your community so that you can present a united front when you approach school administrators. Use organizations already in place—

I FEEL SUGAR-FREE
I feel Sugar-Free.
Would you be Sugar-Free with me?
I'm in good shape.
I look like this because I eat right.
I look good and great.
Yes! Yes!
Finally I'm glad to be me.
I have lots of energy
To run, to jump, to play and spin.
I feel good, good this way.
Yes! Yes!
Now, look, I'm Sugar-Free.
You should be
Sugar-Free with me.

—*Charles, second grade*

---

the PTA, other community groups interested in health and fitness. If possible, ally with medical and health professionals whose children attend your children's school; whether it's fair or not, the opinions of doctors, nutritionists, and dieticians may carry more weight.

• Use the Internet to gather information on government programs that may provide funding to assist your school or school district in making the transition to healthier menus.

• Create a resource library that other families can use. Include healthy cookbooks, store information for suppliers of healthy products, and even maps to help people find farm stands and organic produce purveyors.

• Offer your services. Give a cooking workshop, or organize trips to health food stores for parents who may feel insecure about shopping for unfamiliar products.

• Gather the ammunition that you need to win over the school board, the county supervisors, and anyone who is involved in the decision-making process.

- Use the press! If a local TV or newspaper reporter sends children to your school, you can expect to get the kind of coverage that may speed results.

- Keep trying. It may take time to create the kinds of changes you want to see in your schools and community. But never forget: your children deserve it, and the results of your efforts will be worth it!

Resources and Support

Finding the Help You Need

_____

Because so many people now have Internet access, I want to give you a few sites to get you started since one of the best ways to get involved is doing your own research. Only you know what products you and your family will like, and only you can choose the flavors and products you will most enjoy trying.

Here are some user-friendly sites that I think will bring the best of healthy and organic products to you, no matter where you live!

(Please note that sometimes site names change or sites are taken down. I have tried to make sure that the following recommendations will be there for you.)

Sources for Products
www.countrychoicenaturals.com
Organic cookies, cereals, and hot cocoas.

www.ediblenature.com
Organic energy bars, health and wellness superstore.

www.edwardandsons.com
Organic confections, soups, crackers, terrific sauces.

www.shopnatural.com
Groceries and pet-care supplies to beauty items and vitamins.

www.stretch-island.com
Fruit leathers.

www.vitalicious.com
VitaMuffins and VitaTops (muffin tops). Check out sugar-free/low-carb banana nut and chocolate.

www.lightlife.com
A terrific line of soy products, including Smart Meals on-the-Go, single servings of chili, barbeque, and Tex-Mex you just heat and eat.

Sources for Information and Support
www.diabetes.org
American Diabetes Association's home page.

www.Diabetic-Lifestyle.com
You don't have to be a diabetic to love this Web site, which is rich with ideas and information to help you live a healthier lifestyle. Recipes, health updates, nutrition data, and even a special section for kids.

www.obesity.org/subs/childhood
Information on childhood obesity from the American Obesity Association.

www.Kidnetic.com
Fun family nutrition site, with games, quizzes, recipes.

www.KidsHealth.com
Created by the Nemours Foundation's Center for Children's Health Media. Most visited site on the Web providing doctor-approved health information. Separate sections for kids, teens, and parents.

www.SmartMouth.org
Sponsored by the Center for Science in the Public Interest. Offers recipes, articles, "snacktoids," and more.

www.nutritionexplorations.org
Created by the National Dairy Council. Features nutrition information for educators and parents.

www.nutritioustable.com
Some good advice for families on healthy eating from a registered dietician.

www.usda.gov/news/usdakids
The U.S. Department of Agriculture for Kids with nutrition guidelines, conservation tips, children's activities, gardening advice, 4-H information, and kids' science projects.

www.nutrition.gov
Up-to-the-minute nutrition and fitness news from the U.S. government.

www.fns.usda.gov/tn/
The site for Team Nutrition, an initiative of the USDA Food and Nutrition Service designed to support the Child Nutrition Programs through training and technical assistance for food service, nutrition education for children and their caregivers, and school and community support for healthy eating and physical activity.

www.fns.usda.gov/tn/Healthy/index.htm
USDA site for Healthy Schools resources.

www.eatright.org
American Dietetic Association provides food and nutrition information and healthy products. Also provides information on National Nutrition Month.

www.homefoodsafety.org
American Dietetic Association education site funded by ConAgra education grants. Gives tips on kitchen safety and on home food safety.

www.pe4life.com
This nonprofit's mission is to inspire "active, healthy living by advancing the development of quality, daily physical education programs for all children."

www.kidsource.com
A great site with links to much useful info for parents—"In-depth & timely education & healthcare information that will make a difference in the lives of parents & children."

www.take10.net
TAKE10!® is a "classroom-based physical activity program for kindergarten to fifth-grade students, a curriculum tool created by teachers for teachers and students." TAKE 10!® offers "safe and age-appropriate 10-minute physical activities."

www.educationworld.com
Great site for lesson plans on all subjects, including health and nutrition.

www.projectfitamerica.org
Dedicated to getting kids fit since 1990, this is a national nonprofit public charity that donates to schools, grades K–12, providing fully funded cardiovascular health and lifetime fitness education programs. Information on grants, equipment, activities, and more.

www.cdc.gov/HealthyYouth/physicalactivity
From the Centers for Disease Control, a lot of research and strategies for parents and schools on the subject of physical fitness and children's health.

www.dole5aday.com
Sponsored by Dole Pineapple, this site provides nutrition information and activities sections for kids, teachers, and parents.

**www.childdevelopmentinfo.com/health_safety/physical_
fitness_guide_for_kids.htm**
Provides the Physical Fitness Guide for Kids and Teens from Child Development Institute. (Source: American Medical Association and American Academy of Pediatrics.)

Appendix:Dietary Guidelines for Americans

Some Key Recommendations for the General Population, Published January 12, 2005

Weight Management

- To maintain body weight in a healthy range, balance calories from foods and beverages with calories expended.

- To prevent gradual weight gain over time, make small decreases in food and beverage calories and increase physical activity.

Physical Activity

- Engage in regular physical activity and reduce sedentary activities to promote health, psychological well-being, and a healthy body weight.

- To reduce the risk of chronic disease in adulthood, engage in at least thirty minutes of moderate-intensity physical activity, above usual activity, at work or home on most days of the week.

- For most people, greater health benefits can be obtained by engaging in physical activity of more vigorous intensity or longer duration.

- To help manage body weight and prevent gradual, unhealthy body weight gain in adulthood, engage in approximately sixty minutes of moderate- to vigorous-intensity activity on most days of the week while not exceeding caloric intake requirements.

• To sustain weight loss in adulthood, participate in at least sixty to ninety minutes of daily moderate-intensity physical activity while not exceeding caloric intake requirements. Some people may need to consult with a health-care provider before participating in this level of activity.

• Achieve physical fitness by including cardiovascular conditioning, stretching exercises for flexibility, and resistance exercises or calisthenics for muscle strength and endurance.

Adequate Nutrients within Calorie Needs

• Consume a variety of nutrient-dense foods and beverages within and among the basic food groups while choosing foods that limit the intake of saturated and trans fats, cholesterol, added sugars, salt, and alcohol.

• Meet recommended intakes within energy needs by adopting a balanced eating pattern, such as the U.S. Department of Agriculture (USDA) food guide or the Dietary Approaches to Stop Hypertension (DASH) eating plan.

Food Groups to Encourage

• Consume a sufficient amount of fruits and vegetables while staying within energy needs. Two cups of fruit and two-and-a-half cups of vegetables per day are recommended for a two-thousand-calorie intake.

• Choose a variety of fruits and vegetables each day. In particular, select from all five vegetable subgroups (dark green, orange, legumes, starchy vegetables, and other vegetables) several times a week.

• Consume three or more ounce-equivalents of whole-grain products per day, with the rest of the recommended grains coming from enriched or whole-grain products. In general, at least half the grains should come from whole grains.

• Consume three cups per day of fat-free or low-fat milk or equivalent milk products.

Food Safety

• Clean hands, food contact surfaces, and fruits and vegetables. Meat and poultry should not be washed or rinsed to avoid spreading bacteria to other foods.

• Separate raw, cooked, and ready-to-eat foods while shopping, preparing, or storing foods.

• Cook foods to a safe temperature to kill microorganisms.

• Chill (refrigerate) perishable food promptly and defrost foods properly.

• Avoid raw (unpasteurized) milk or any products made from unpasteurized milk, raw or partially cooked eggs or foods containing raw eggs, or raw or undercooked meat and poultry, unpasteurized juices, and raw sprouts.

Fats

• Consume less than 10 percent of calories from saturated fatty acids and less than three hundred milligrams per day of cholesterol, and keep trans-fatty acid consumption as low as possible.

• Keep total fat intake between 20 to 35 percent of calories, with most fats coming from sources of polyunsaturated and monounsaturated fatty acids, such as fish, nuts, and vegetable oils.

• When selecting and preparing meat, poultry, dry beans, and milk or milk products, make choices that are lean, low-fat, or fat-free.

• Limit intake of fats and oils high in saturated and/or trans-fatty acids, and choose products low in such fats and oils.

Carbohydrates

• Choose fiber-rich fruits, vegetables, and whole grains often.

• Choose and prepare foods and beverages with little added sugars or caloric sweeteners, such as amounts suggested by the USDA food guide and the DASH eating plan.

• Reduce the incidence of dental caries by practicing good oral hygiene and consuming sugar- and starch-containing foods and beverages less frequently.

Sodium and Potassium

• Consume less than twenty-three hundred milligrams (approximately one teaspoon of salt) of sodium per day.

• Choose and prepare foods with little salt. At the same time, consume potassium-rich foods, such as fruits and vegetables.

The complete text of the 2005 Guidelines can be accessed on the web at http://www.health.gov/dietaryguidelines/.

Acknowledgments

I have been a dreamer all of my life, and it has been through those dreams that I know that anything is possible. However, it has been only by God's grace that I have been able to make those dreams come true. I am proud and honored to give thanks to some very special people who have supported me through this wonderful journey.

Ruthie Mae Sanders was not only my mother but my friend. I am the woman I am today largely because of her tireless hours of support, love, and faith in me. Mom, I will always love and miss you. S. W.

Floyd, my husband and friend: you have continued to make sacrifices to ensure that my dreams became reality. I love you, guy!

Denard, my son: you encourage me and love me in spite of my missing your rodeo finals to meet deadlines for my book. Love you, dude!

West Sanders, my Daddy Bo: your struggles and sacrifices as a father secured the futures of my siblings and me. You will always be my hero. I love you more.

My sisters, the Fantastic Six: Dorothy, Lillie, Shirley, Doris, Betty, and Annette. Thanks for encouraging me and loving me through this entire process. Love & Kisses.

Dannie, my best girlfriend and sister: there are no words to express our relationship. Love U Girl!

Mary Young, one of my dearest friends: your love and spiritual guidance has continued to keep me focused. Thank you.

John Duff, my publisher, for whom I have genuine respect: from the first day we spoke, you made me feel comfortable with this business and made me feel that I had a story that needed to be told. With your guidance and support, it is happening. Thank you for having confidence in me.

Barbara Alpert, a very gifted educator and writer, who helped me to express a message for which I had very strong and passionate feelings. You are the best!

Lorine Bizzell, my nutritionist and dietician, who has supported me through it all. Thank you, my friend.

The Ennovy family: Thaddeus, Nekita, Hazel, Shellay, Tan, and Curtis. What would I do without you guys? Well, I won't ever have to know (LOL).

Jim and Andy: a million thanks to two excellent advisors and visionaries. Your support is priceless.

Last but not least, love and thanks to the kids, parents, and staff at Browns Mill School, who have been my inspiration and support throughout this entire process.

Index